"*Bring Me the Rhinoceros* is one of the best books ever written about Zen."

—STEPHEN MITCHELL, translator of
Gilgamesh: A New English Version

"Here's a book to crack the happiness code if ever there was one. Forget about self-improvement, five-point plans, and inspirational seminars that you can't remember a word of a week later. Tarrant's is the fix that fixes nothing because there is nothing to fix. Your life is a koan, a deep question whose answer you are already living—this is the true inspiration, and Tarrant delivers."

—ROGER HOUSDEN, author of the Ten Poems series

"Every life is full of koans, and yet you can't learn from a book how to understand them. You need someone to put you in the right frame of mind to see the puzzles and paradoxes of your experience. With intelligence, humor, and steady deep reflection, John Tarrant does this as no one has done it before. This book could take you to a different and important level of experience."

—THOMAS MOORE, author of *Care of the Soul*

"John Tarrant's talent for telling these classic Zen tales transforms them magically into a song in which, as you read, the words disappear as the music continues to echo in the your mind and make you happy. Mysteriously, like koans."

—SYLVIA BOORSTEIN, author of
Pay Attention, For Goodness' Sake

BRING ME THE RHINOCEROS

and Other Zen Koans That Will Save Your Life

JOHN TARRANT

SHAMBHALA • *Boston & London* • 2008

Shambhala Publications, Inc.
Horticultural Hall
300 Massachusetts Avenue
Boston, Massachusetts 02115
www.shambhala.com

Updated edition of *Bring Me the Rhinoceros:
And Other Zen Koans to Bring You Joy*
originally published by Harmony Books.

Excerpt from "Per Diem" from *Shroud of the Gnome*
© 1997 by James Tate. Reprinted by permission of
HarperCollins Publishers Inc.
Excerpt from "Botany Bay" from *In Possession of a Cow*
by Alicia Keane. Reprinted by permission of author.
Excerpt from "My Dead Friends" from *What the Living Do*
by Marie Howe. © 1997 by Marie Howe.
Used by permission of W. W. Norton & Company, Inc.

9 8 7 6 5 4 3 2

Printed in the United States of America

♾ This edition is printed on acid-free paper that meets
the American National Standards Institute z39.48 Standard.
♻ This book was printed on 30% postconsumer recycled paper.
For more information please visit www.shambhala.com.
Distributed in the United States by Random House, Inc.,
and in Canada by Random House of Canada Ltd

LIBRARY OF CONGRESS CATALOGING-IN-PUBLICATION DATA
Tarrant, John, 1949–
Bring me the rhinoceros: and other Zen koans that will save your life /
John Tarrant.
    p. cm.
Includes bibliographical references.
ISBN 978-1-59030-618-5 (pbk.: alk. paper)
1. Koan. I. Title.
BQ9289.5.T373 2008
294.3'4432—dc22
2008017136

FOR JOAN

Contents

Acknowledgments

This book is a report on using koans as a way of transformation in the modern world. One of the features of the project is an open culture of collaboration—many hands and hearts have been at work here.

Thanks to Michael Katz, for conceiving the book, Joan Sutherland, for reimagining koans, editing, and translation, and Byron Katie for her approach to inquiry.

For years, Rachel Howlett, Brian Howlett, David Weinstein, Lyn Bouguereau, and Michelle Riddle have given material generously and collaborated to develop the ideas in this book.

Others who have helped are Susan Murphy, Stephen Mitchell, Ken Ireland, Jon Joseph, Joe Mancuso, Alan Williamson, Rachel Boughton, Mayumi Oda, Rachael Flannery, Roberta Goldfarb, Richie Domingue, Seraphina Goldfarb-Tarrant, Michael Sierchio, Julian Gresser, Alison Ellett, Ann Hunkins, Linda Brown, Bill Krumbein, Paul Abrahamsen, Tom McConnell, and James Anthony. Thanks. Pacific Zen Institute has given me a home base. Tracy Gaudet and Duke Integrative Medicine provide a proving ground for ideas about transforming consciousness. Wolf Creek Partners also provides a way of implementing these ideas in health care and medicine.

BRING ME THE RHINOCEROS

Introduction

This book offers an unusual path into happiness. It doesn't encourage you to strive for things or manipulate people or change yourself into an improved, more polished version of you. Instead, it suggests a way to approach happiness indirectly by unbuilding, unmaking, tossing overboard, and generally subverting unhappiness. And even this indirect approach is not based on a plan. It's hard to plan for something that takes you beyond what you can imagine, which is what this method is designed to do. The method described in this book is based on Zen koans ("ko-an") and has been in use for a long time in East Asia, though in the United States, Europe, and Australia it is just getting established. The goal of the Zen koan is enlightenment, which is a profound change of heart. This change of heart makes the world seem like a different place; with it comes a freedom of mind and an awareness of the joy and kindness underlying daily life.

Koans are not intended to prescribe a particular kind of happiness or right way to live. They don't teach you to assemble or make something that didn't exist before. Many psychological and spiritual approaches rely on an engineering metaphor and hope to make your mind more predictable and controllable. Koans go the other way. They encourage you to make an ally of the unpredictability of the mind and to approach your life more as a work of art. The surprise they offer is the one that art offers: inside unpredictability you will find not chaos, but beauty. Koans light up a life that may have been dormant in you; they hold out the possibility of transformation even if you are trying to address unclear or apparently insoluble problems.

To begin with, here are seven things to notice about koans:

Koans show you that you can depend on creative moves. Usually people think of a creative leap as something like one, two, three, four . . . six. With koans a creative leap is more like one, two, three, four . . . rhinoceros. What if happiness were a creative activity, like writing a poem? You cannot know where the next line of a poem will come from and you can't force it, yet there is a discipline that helps. When you attend in the right way, the poem's next line really does arrive out of nowhere. In the same way, through a koan, happiness can arrive out of nowhere.

Koans encourage doubt and curiosity. Koans don't ask you to believe anything offensive to reason. You can have any religion and use koans. You can have no religion and use koans. Koans don't take away painful beliefs and put positive beliefs in their place. Koans just take away the painful beliefs and so provide freedom. What you do with that freedom is up to you.

Koans rely on uncertainty as a path to happiness. If you set off after happiness thinking that you know what you need, you will always end up with something that meets that need. The problem here is that when you are unhappy, it is as if you are in prison, and in that narrow cell you think of happiness with an inmate's mind. You might imagine a more comfy cell, consider painting the walls a nicer color—rose, perhaps—and getting a new sofa. Koans don't support the interior decoration project; they demolish the walls.

Koans will undermine your reasons and your explanations. If you have a reason for happiness, then that happiness can be taken away. The person you love could leave, the job could stop being interesting. If you have a reason for loving life, what happens if that reason fails? With koans you may find that life and love are so strong and vivid that they can't be explained or justified. Koans open a happiness that comes for no good reason. That happiness exists before reasons have appeared in the universe.

Koans lead you to see life as funny rather than tragic. Well, which would you rather? This is one of their delights. For example, an earnest visitor asked a Chinese master, "Where do we go when we die?"

"I shall go straight to hell," said the old master.

"You?" said the questioner, "A good Zen master, why would you go to hell?"

"If I don't, who will teach you?"

Koans will change your idea of who you are, and this will require courage. If you are used to living in a small room and suddenly discover a wide meadow, you might feel unsafe. Everyone thinks that they want happiness, but they might not. They might rather keep their stories about who they are and about what is impossible. Happiness is not an add-on to what you already are; it requires you to become a different person from the one who set off seeking it.

Koans uncover a hidden kindness in life. Koans show a path in which kindness is part of the foundation of the mind; not one of its accoutrements, nor something to be cultivated. If it were an attainment, kindness could be taken away or lost. When you unpack all your motives and other people's motives and get to the bottom of things, you find love. I know that this is a shocking thing to say but I will try to show you how it is true.

STUMBLING INTO KOANS

At twenty-two I was an occasional secretary and live-in gardener to the Australian poet Judith Wright. In her garden, butterflies swirled; satin bowerbirds built bowers and danced with flowers and blue clothes pegs in their beaks; lorikeets and small wallabies passed through on their separate roads. At the foot of the paddock the leftover rainforest began—great festooned trees hanging in the sky like branching neurons. When the neighbor died, his wife buried him down by the creek and dared the timidly inquiring police to find him. I had a desk in the basement, and bush rats ran over my toes. The hallucinatory mushrooms I occasionally took seemed hardly necessary to make life more numinous.

Still, there were questions that would not go away. None of the usual solutions to life that were on offer meant much to me and, like many young people, I didn't at first expect to live for a long time. When I continued living anyway and needed to make a life, I found myself yearning to make sense of things. I had noticed, as almost everyone does, moments of great and apparently everlasting beauty followed by standard-issue miseries and found the incongruence hard to deal with. I wanted to be loyal to that beauty while not dodging the dark bits.

"But what is the universe made of?" I asked. "How does it all go together? Can it come apart? What are we doing here?" It seems odd now that I didn't ask, "Why are we unhappy?" Perhaps I took happiness as secondary, a corollary of answering the "what's it all about?" questions. My question was urgent, but I wasn't sure what it was. I wasn't certain if I had one question or many. And I didn't want an answer in the conventional sense. Instead, I wanted a magic key to a realm in which the insoluble, and even indefinable, questions made sense. One of the good things about Judith Wright was that, while she was herself passionately involved in the outer, political tumult of that time—over war and Aboriginal land rights and saving the Great Barrier Reef—she knew immediately what I meant.

"You probably need to go to India for that," she said, without apparent irony, and turned back to her typewriter. It was as if I had asked where she kept the paper clips.

"Oh," I said, slightly let down. I had hoped she might be able to tell me herself.

I took her reply to mean that for certain kinds of knowledge you have to undertake a journey. It isn't like pouring water into a bucket—a process by which neither water nor bucket is much changed. It seemed that if I took this journey I would be utterly changed. And before setting out, I couldn't predict what that change would be. That was interesting to me. It encouraged me to set off with only the vaguest directions.

It might give plausibility to my account to say that I was led to koans by a blinding flash, but I just stumbled across them in a book. They looked to be a kind of Chinese poetry. It was at a time when managing my mind had come to seem like a really good idea, and I needed a method. I knew immediately that koans might help. It was as if I held out my hand to see if it was raining and a yellow ball fell into my palm. I didn't understand the koans, but they made my life seem beautiful, even the painful and miserable parts, and that changed the value of everything.

When I was off balance, koans pushed me further off balance and into unknown territory. I liked that. I was always struggling to have things make sense, and koans allowed me, or required me, to work with life more the way an artist would, loving especially the material that didn't make sense. They were keys to another realm where even serious problems had a different and lesser valence.

I read and worked on koans by myself and then traveled to study with teachers of the koan schools. Eventually I worked to make the method user-friendly, because koans are something I love and I thought others might find them helpful too. I wrote this book so you can try the method and see if you like it.

What Are Koans Exactly?

When I tried to find out what koans are, it became clear that *koan* is a Japanese word that has entered the English language without bringing a clear sense of its meaning. It is usually taken to refer to some sort of riddle or odd question. A koan actually has its origin in sayings or records of conversations between people interested in the secret of life.

Koans originated when Chinese culture flowered about thirteen hundred years ago, at the period of the Arthurian legends in England. In China it was a time of willow pattern ceramics, wood block printing, great poets and painters, and, just as in Europe, civil war. It was also a time when people grew seriously interested in the technology of the mind. Certain spiritual teachers became known for a deep and free understanding of life, and people came to learn, hoping to gain the insight that a teacher had. Some left farms, homes, and jobs in the bureaucracy to form monastic communities; some traveled a thousand miles on foot. These students worked, studied, meditated, and asked questions. Others maintained their work and family life and dropped in for periods of study. The teachers weren't trying to achieve something; they just responded to the needs of their students, and it turned out that some of their improvised decisions kept the process interesting.

First of all, they trusted doubt and rewarded questions. This is rare in religion and an example of the Zen way of treating what is usually thought of as a problem—in this case, doubt—as a strength.

The teachers also treated all questions as if they were relevant, no matter what their content. "Why did I lose my love?" would have the same spiritual value as "What happens when I die?" A question is a place of embarkation, and any question was treated as being about enlightenment, whether the student was aware of it or not. There was a trust in whatever forces had brought the student to the point of asking.

Finally, instead of giving kind advice, or step-by-step instructions, the teachers responded to the students as if they were capable of coming to a complete understanding in that moment. A teacher's words often made no rational sense, yet possessed a strangely compelling quality. For example, someone had this exchange with a great teacher:

"I am Qingshui, alone and destitute. Please help me."

Caoshan said, "Mr. Shui!"

"Yes!"

Caoshan said, "You have already drunk three cups of the finest wine, and yet you say that you haven't even wet your lips."

Of all the answers the student might have been hoping for, he probably wasn't expecting to be involved in a call and response and to be told that he was rich. Yet, when you think you are desolate, it can be an intriguing and hopeful thing to be told that you are not. After such exchanges, a student who had been stuck and unhappy might be suddenly full of joy. More often, the words would work away in the mind, gradually drawing the student out of a limiting view he or she held.

Some exchanges became famous and were written down. They came to be known as koans—the word means "public case"—and there was a mania for collecting them. A well-known teacher forbade his students to write down what he said because he thought people were recording his comments as a substitute for the more necessary and dangerous task of letting them work on the mind. One man adapted by wearing paper clothing to lectures, and the notes he jotted down secretly on his sleeves were passed around. These koans in turn became the core of one of the great koan collections, *The Blue Cliff Record*.

Soldiers, housewives, farmers, and merchants used koans to find freedom within the often difficult conditions of their times. The method was to immerse yourself in the saying and see how it changed you. This meant letting the koan teach you by interacting with your life and your mind; the activity wasn't confined to periods of formal meditation. People farmed the land, ran bureaucracies, and raised children, all the while keeping moment-by-moment company with their koan.

In one instance, when Genghis Khan's troops swept through China in the twelfth century, provincial governors went to the Khan and became senior ministers. They lived out on the steppes with him, hoping to persuade him to rule the cities rather than burning them and converting them into horse pasture. It would be hard not to feel unprepared for, and perhaps terrified of, such a task, and one of the ministers asked his teacher for advice. The most helpful thing the teacher could think of was to make a collection of koans and poems that he called the *Book of Serenity*. When this book arrived on the steppes, the story goes, the ministers sat up together all night in a yurt, reading the koans aloud. They had an impossible situation, so they saturated themselves in a method that prepared them to take advantage of whatever tiniest possibility might indeed appear.

Today it is not so different from the way it was in China. People are called on to survive terror attacks and random mayhem. And even the most domestic life has its quota of desperation and insoluble problems and its requirements for unusual kindness. Today people can find koans as helpful as they did long ago.

Each chapter of this book has a koan and some comments on it. The koan in its original form is given separately on the opening page of the chapter. The comments on the koan vary. Sometimes they show you how you might enjoy working with the koan. Sometimes they give an account of a person's experience working with the koan, and that person might be ancient or recent. And sometimes they show situations and attitudes that make most sense in terms of the koan style of thinking, which will become clearer as we go along.

And as for me, did I go to India to answer my questions, as my mentor suggested long ago? Well, not literally. As it turned out, India, strangely enough, came to me, without my asking, in the form of koans. Chapter 1 opens a gate into those questions by taking up one of the oldest of the koan stories.

1

Bodhidharma's Vast Emptiness

Emperor Wu of Liang asked the great master Bodhidharma,

"What is the main point of this holy teaching?"

"Vast emptiness, nothing holy," said Bodhidharma.

"Who are you, standing in front of me?" asked the emperor.

"I do not know," said Bodhidharma.

The emperor didn't understand. Bodhidharma crossed the Yangtze River and went to the kingdom of Wei.

Later, the emperor raised this matter with his advisor, Duke Zhi. The advisor asked,

"Your Majesty, do you know who that Indian sage was?"

"No I don't," said the emperor.

"That was Avalokiteshvara, the Bodhisattva of Compassion, carrying the seal of the Buddha's heart and mind."

The emperor felt a sudden regret and said, "Send a messenger to call him back."

Duke Zhi told him, "Your Majesty, even if everyone in the kingdom went after him he wouldn't return."

FORGETTING WHO YOU ARE
AND MAKING USE OF NOTHING

To study the Buddha's way is to study the self,
to study the self is to forget the self.
To forget the self is to be awakened
by ten thousand things.

—Eihei Dogen

Poetry arrived
to look for me. I don't know, I don't know where
it came from, from winter or river,
I don't know how or when,
No there weren't voices, there weren't words, or silence.

—Pablo Neruda

IF YOU ARE IN A TIGHT SPOT and nothing has worked, you prob-ably think that you need a transcendent piece of wisdom to rely on. You might think that you need a foothold or a handhold. You might think that you need to improve yourself or your skills in some way. Here is a koan that suggests another possibility: the way through might be by not improving yourself and not finding a railing to take hold of. Here is a koan about how the way through can appear naturally if you are open to it taking an unfamiliar shape. This koan also contains the legend about how this understanding was brought to China from India.

THE KOAN

Bodhidharma's Vast Emptiness

Emperor Wu had two unusual experiences that changed his life. These essentially inward events led him to certain achievements that are remembered today, more than a millennium after his death. The first experience happened when his armies had to repel an invasion of horsemen from the northwest. The horsemen carried with them whatever they owned, and they weren't afraid to die. The emperor had himself ascended to the throne in the standard way, by overthrowing the previous, weakened monarch, and he believed that he understood the riders. To steady his troops he visited the front lines and sat in the firelight on a small hill. This is when the emperor had his first peculiar experience.

Banners whipped loudly overhead and the wind felt as though it were inside his chest, tearing and banging. Something of the desert's tedious immensity was conveyed to him. The wind cleansed him of any anxiety and also took away other things the solidity of which he had never questioned before. It took away his august rank and his name. He stopped planning, and he also stopped thinking about the outcome of the battle. When everything he usually depended upon was gone, he knew immediately what to do. In the predawn, just before the nomads liked to attack, he sent horsemen into the center of their camp and immediately pulled them back again. As the pursuit came, the center of his line kept falling back. The nomads rode into the vacuum he had opened and he closed on them from both sides.

After his return, while the ministers celebrated, the emperor went into the garden to be alone. On the hillside, he had felt quite certain that he was going to win. At that moment, in the wind and the vast land, he was small and unimportant, and this sense of his unimportance allowed him to be clear about what needed to be done. Being important now seemed to him to be just a prejudice that confined him.

Once he forgot about having a special point to his life, he felt remarkably free for an emperor. There were some complications. On certain days he considered leaving his room but couldn't find a reason to. He still gave interviews at court before dawn but was sometimes beset by a sense of unreality. Shedding his old beliefs had not been so hard. He hadn't done anything to achieve his new way of seeing things; it was a gift from wind and war. Having opinions about life—ideas about being an emperor, about his own dignity and the motives of his ministers, having to dislike this person and admire that one—pained him now; he could feel these familiar attitudes as walls crowding around him. Yet some understanding, he was certain, eluded him. He did what was necessary out of duty and didn't mourn his old certainties, but he lacked delight. There had to be more to life than the freedom of pointlessness.

The emperor sought hints from the world. He noticed that he had remorse about the murders involved in his ascent to the throne. His qualms, as he thought of them, were the beginning of a new curiosity about his own life. At the same time he began to entertain famous teachers who passed through. Sometimes they were helpful. They usually praised him and gave carefully bland advice, often involving diets. Sometimes it was even good advice, but the question he had was something like a feeling—a mingling of excitement and uneasiness hard to formulate—and advice didn't seem to touch it.

Then the emperor heard of a sage from India. The man was himself a legend; it was said that it had taken him three years to make his way over the seas. The emperor knew nothing about the sea, but he imagined waves as the grass of the steppes in a high wind. He tried thinking of China as an ocean that he passed through, and nomads as pirates with horses. Though his own obligations prevented him from undertaking such journeys, he respected this kind of solitary accomplishment.

When this sage arrived at court, he turned out to be a genuine barbarian: red hair, blue eyes, dressed in rags. His name was Bodhidharma, which was not really a personal name, just some sort of title in Sanskrit. The clothes of the ministers were gorgeous, and in the red-and-gold audience room the visitor managed to seem nondescript, which was an achievement for a barbarian. He didn't have the air of one deprived or poor; the main contrast with the ministers was not in how he dressed. In a place where everyone wanted something, he did not. The ministers' rank was displayed by differences in insignia and dress; the sage made no claims about rank. He didn't either push himself forward into the emperor's notice or pull himself back into hiding. He stood quietly, and his presence affected the court until everyone fell silent. The emperor noticed that his own thoughts were becoming simple; he remembered the taste of vegetable soup.

"Even the most elegant palace," thought the emperor, "is also a burden." Then he stood up as if to approach the visitor's stillness. He wanted to find a road deeper into his own life, and asked, "I have funded many monasteries; what merit have I earned?"

"No merit," said Bodhidharma.

With a jolt, the emperor thought, "Here is someone who knows! It's not about building things up. It's about undoing everything." He realized that he had fallen into being an emperor again and underestimated the sage and perhaps himself. He had not dared to ask a question important to his own life. The memory of a hillside and a battle rose up in him. He had had no language for what he had undergone, had had no one to stand beside him and say, "Yes, I see it too!" Now the emperor felt the man's presence as a kind of sympathy, which he longed to explore.

"What is the main point of this holy teaching?"

"Vast emptiness, nothing holy," said Bodhidharma.

Again the quiet voice that didn't ask to be heard. The emperor's senses became keen. It was as if the two men were sitting together on a bench in a temple garden with all the time in the world. He wanted to reach the other man's mind, or perhaps go deeper into his own mind. An odd thought came to him: "If I'm an emperor, how can I also be a person?" So he asked, "Who are you, standing in front of me?"

"I do not know," said Bodhidharma.

This statement stopped the emperor completely. He began to feel a delightful insubstantiality. The emperor's sadness over the shameful things he had done fell away, it fell into that emptiness. The emperor's worry over when more attacks would come from the north also disappeared. Inside himself he couldn't find an emperor.

He felt capable of many things but not quite yet; the words "I don't know, I don't know" stuck in his head like a line from a song. For a moment, he walked alone and was content. Around him, emptiness flowed in all directions. Then, as he looked about, the palace returned and the court officials started to whisper to each other. He was fascinated by how clear everything was. Someone else spoke, and Bodhidharma began to withdraw, as if he were himself a spell that had been lifted. If he had stayed, "I don't know" might have lost its power. In the court, only one person noted his going.

Later, the emperor raised this matter with his advisor, Duke Zhi. The advisor asked, "Your Majesty, do you know who that Indian sage was?"

"No, I don't," said the emperor, realizing how much emperors take for granted.

"That was Avalokiteshvara, the Bodhisattva of Compassion, carrying the seal of the Buddha's heart and mind."

The emperor felt a sudden regret and said, "Send a messenger to call him back."

Duke Zhi told him, "Your Majesty, even if everyone in the kingdom went after him he wouldn't return."

"I met him but didn't meet him," said the emperor, and eventually those words were put on his grave. This was his way of expressing his own "I don't know."

Afterward the emperor noticed more about his own life. He noticed that when he didn't expect people to please him, he enjoyed seeing them. That seemed to be a clue. He found that he enjoyed building temples; it wasn't a matter of duty. Then he went further. The emperor gave himself up to temples as a slave, seeking inward freedom in an exterior narrowness, in forgetting how to be an emperor. At such times he felt full of love. He dug ditches and planted gardens. He wasn't an emperor or a murderer; the work took away his sense of himself. Like the Indian sage, he didn't know who he was and was free until he became himself again. The strategy was also an excellent fundraising device for the temples, since the game was that his ministers had to ransom him with huge gifts. And he enjoyed tormenting his ministers in this mild way. After he was ransomed he would live contentedly in the palace for a while until a feeling of suffocation and surfeit became once more unendurable, and he would give himself up to a temple and be a gardener once more.

Bodhidharma went away without carrying even one opinion about the emperor and sat for nine years in the mountains facing a cliff. "I don't know" continues to murmur, century after century. People wait and live inside questions; mistakes lead through doors. The idea that there is a wisdom that the universe just gives to you without reference to teachers or scriptures came from Bodhidharma to the reader of this page and is happening right now.

Working with the Koan

A man is madly in love one day and the next cares only to go fishing. A country goes to great lengths to make an alliance and within a year has changed sides. This is not just fickleness and greed. There is an insubstantiality to human reasons and motives and identity. You may make an expedition to meet people in loincloths as photographed by *National Geographic* but find that they have copies of the article with them, and have taken to wearing Nikes and T-shirts with pictures of hip-hop artists on them.

What we believe about ourselves does not stand up to examination, so there is always the problem of describing our own lives in a plausible way. The old teachers named this insubstantiality "emptiness." They thought that, contrary to the medieval idea that something cannot come out of nothing, everything we do comes out of nothing.

Occasionally, awakening from sleep you may wonder, "Where on earth am I?" Or, fleetingly, in a more disoriented awakening, the question becomes, "Who am I?" or even, "What am I?" These moments, when you open your eyes in the world as if for the first time, like a newborn, can be delicious. With the uncertainty comes a feeling of freedom.

In the Zen tradition, you are asked about Bodhidharma's three answers: "No merit," "Vast emptiness," and "I do not know." One place to start is with the idea of no merit.

No merit. How much do you do for praise? How many things do you say just to make an impression on others? What are you really achieving when you try to make an impression? And how many accounts do you have to keep? If you didn't do things for merit and advancement, or if you didn't act with motives at all, what would life be like? At work? In bed? Alone in a room? Even alone in a room you can be consumed with wanting other people to see you in a good light. Can you imagine how things would be without that kind of wanting?

Vast emptiness, nothing holy. What is the mind like if it's not occupied with plans and schemes, and fears that the plans and schemes will fail? What if your unexamined beliefs were to fall away and you were to live without them, and also to live without the thought that you had given anything up?

I don't know. If you were to put aside what you know because of what other people told you, how much of what you know do you truly know for yourself? If you look for the origin of your thoughts, of your life, of your universe, can you find it? Can you find where this moment comes from or where it goes home to?

Driving home from a retreat in the redwoods, I come into the small town of Occidental and, seeing shops and houses, realize, "Oh, the twenty-first century." But because I have spent a week forgetting what to expect and indeed forgetting who I am, I wouldn't be shocked if it was any century.

A friend who is curious about the way the mind works for happiness or unhappiness spent an afternoon with a Hindu teacher. During their conversation, he asked the teacher, somewhat rhetorically, "Don't you know for sure at least that you are a human being?"

The teacher replied, "In part."

This was not the response my friend expected. His train of thought stopped, and he considered whether he himself knew for sure he was a human being. A gratifying silence enveloped him, and he realized that he had left the conversation hanging. Looking up, he saw the teacher laughing.

Not knowing can be liberating. The same friend is married to a woman with children from a previous marriage. One morning her young son came out in his pajamas and said, "I have a terrible headache."

Immediately the boy's mother said, "Perhaps it's because you ate too much ice cream last night."

Straightaway the man said, "Perhaps it's because you didn't eat enough ice cream last night."

Everyone laughed because either statement could have been

true or untrue. Not knowing why the boy had a headache, every-one felt free.

The old teachers thought that not to know is to step into life without repeating yourself. It is to forget the prejudices and com-parisons that say, "I'm better than you, I'm worse than you, I'm good at this, I'm bad at that." If you practice "don't know" mind for long enough, perhaps you can learn how to be good at anything.

While emptiness is what's left when you take away the thoughts and beliefs that you have constructed around an event, not know-ing is a way to move in the absence of such thoughts. It's a creative possibility. Not knowing who you are allows you to meet an event without pretending it is something else—something that happened before. Then you might experience just what is happening: some-thing unpredictable, delightful, dangerous, safe—eating a taco or walking down the street.

2

Zhaozhou's Dog

Someone asked Zhaozhou, "Does a dog have Buddha nature or not?"

Zhaozhou said, "No."

THE SECRET OF CHANGING
YOUR HEART

I would like to beg you, dear Sir, to have patience with
everything unresolved in your heart and to try to love
the questions themselves as if they were locked rooms or
books written in a very foreign language. Don't search
for the answers, which could not be given to you now,
because you would not be able to live them. And the
point is, to live everything. Live the questions now. Perhaps
then, some day far in the future, you will gradually,
without even noticing it, live your way into the answer.

—RAINER MARIA RILKE'S ADVICE TO A YOUNG POET

KOANS ARE INTENDED to bring about a profound change of
heart, and how does this change come about? It's like what
Hemingway said about going broke: it happens in two ways, "first
slowly, then quickly." The change itself is like walking through a
door. On the other side of that door is the same world you always
knew, yet the eyes you see with are different and this makes it a

new world where new things are possible. It can be hard to express what you have discovered and hard to explain a joy that comes merely from being alive. Yet this change is a real experience that shifts the ground you stand on. One way to put it is that you begin to identify with what was background before. And what you thought of as problems are revealed to be only apparent problems, things in the foreground. In the koan tradition, this discovery was called "intimacy" and considered as a meeting with reality. This chapter will show you a koan typically used to pull people through that door, and give some of the flavor of what it's like to work with that koan. First of all, finding a koan is part of the preparation for working with it, and so legitimately part of the path into the koan. It is as if the koan is beginning to work as you move toward it.

FINDING THE KOAN

I knew that I wanted something without knowing what it was. So I just staggered off in the general direction of what might be helpful. Some Tibetan teachers wandered into Australia, and gave a month-long silent retreat in the hills outside of Brisbane. The place was lush, subtropical, and beloved of mosquitoes. In practice, people had different definitions of silence, so those who thought it meant not talking wore ribbons to identify themselves. I was one of the ribbon-wearing fanatics. The lamas had no clue about Westerners, and we used to meditate for two and a half hours at a time. Yet the discomfort of being with my thoughts was greater than that of being with my body.

One lama played good cop, and talked about how wonderful

enlightenment was. The other lama did bad cop—austere, monastic, prudish—and talked at length about how desire was suffering. He had me imagine how my girlfriend would get old and ugly and die and rot. Also how I would get old, ugly, etc. It seemed to me that while these observations were true, such matters were already well understood and offered little progress toward answering my questions. When people showed signs of distress, the lama introduced the idea of hell realms after death. He was a Christian Brother in fancy dress—some of his words were actually helpful metaphors for the mind's processes, and others seemed merely medieval. I disliked him in a satisfying way. People in the retreat sneaked out to eat meat pies or have love affairs, and although those possibilities were interesting to me, I already knew about them, and I wanted to run into something I didn't know about. That was itself a discovery; I had thought that finding out what was really going on would require a lot of self-denial. Instead, it was more a matter of noticing what I really, really wanted. It was simply more interesting to me than the other options. So I suppose I agreed with the austere lama to the extent that I stuck it out.

One day, as the dislikable lama was teaching about the nature of mind, I unexpectedly found what he was saying to be fascinating. Tears ran down my cheeks. "Ah," I thought, in curiously stilted, deep meditation speak, "this is like being with the sages of the past," and—this took a Christian form for me—I could feel the dust of the Galilee under my shoes, as if I were walking with Jesus on the shore. From then on, I began to take a macabre, Monty Python–like glee in the lama's tales of hell, and to listen more closely to his teachings, though I still didn't like him that much.

What I took away from that experience was the discovery that I wasn't interested in my own opinion of the lama. This was a reversal of the way I had always operated. I could see that what I thought I wanted might not in fact be what I wanted. Then, at that same retreat, I ran across koans in a book and saw that they were related to that sort of reversal. A koan appeals to you the way a song or a poem might. If it is interesting to you in some deep way, then it's for you. The koan that follows is the first koan I worked with. It has been around for a long time and for the last thousand years has been at the top of the charts as a first koan. It is just a fragment of an old story and is really simple.

THE KOAN

Zhaozhou's Dog
Someone asked Zhaozhou, "Does a dog have Buddha nature or not?"
    Zhaozhou said, "No."

WORKING WITH THE KOAN

Zhaozhou was a minimalist. He must have expected his one-word reply to be enough to open the gates of the heart. "The thought that he knew what he was doing," I reasoned, "is more interesting than the opposite." So, what to do with this one word? It is said that once, when Robert Creeley gave a reading as part of a class he was teaching, one of the students asked, "Is that a real poem, or did you make it up yourself?" I had to make up how to work with a koan. The books I read said that you needed a teacher and who knows what mental dangers you would face if you didn't have a teacher and so on. Given that I was in Australia, that sort of advice would have limited me to playing cricket in the bush with kangaroos. Naturally I ignored it.

The dog part of the koan didn't catch me. Cattle dogs of respectable demeanor are welcome in my personal heaven, and Buddha nature just seemed another word for nature, something already sacred. I took the question as, "Does a dog have worth? Do I have worth?—When I'm sick, when I'm ashamed, when I'm bored, when I have no money. Does my friend have worth, and what about my enemy—can I love the whole of life?" I knew that I couldn't love the whole of my life, so that was a promising place to start. Also I didn't mind if my own, hardly coherent wonderings were rolled up into the dog question from a person in his own painful doubt twelve hundred years before. My questions were not any better than his. This made him my comrade.

The one word reply, "No," was easy to concentrate on. One way to work with a koan seemed to be to become completely absorbed in it. This was hard for me at first. The tension of wanting to break through the koan was frustrating, like the tension a child might feel over wanting to ride a bicycle. My face itched and I felt like a failure. I meditated—trying to be unobtrusive—in parks, churches, mountains, trains, the Queensland Parliamentary Library, and the Senate dining room in Canberra. When I sat outside, bush flies (the Australian national bird) crawled into my eye corners, seeking moisture.

Koans required a humility that is really a kind of plainness in approaching life without drama and ulterior motives. I had no great reserves of such humility; it was something that had to appear by itself because I didn't know that it was needed. Gradually

I stopped expecting the kinds of things I usually expected. I didn't know what scale of difficulty was appropriate for my problem, and after a while it didn't seem hard or easy. When I resolved, or rather noticed, that even if I got nowhere with the koan, I would keep with it for the rest of my not-very-important life, that softened my heart a little. It allowed me to just have the meditation I happened to be having, without complaint. I was lobbying for Aboriginal land rights at the time and meetings were often held in pubs, so I learned to meditate drunk and then learned how boring my mind was when I was drunk. My idea was to meditate no matter what.

A few years later found me at dawn whacking a large Japanese hanging bell with a wooden mallet. Down its sides the bell had bronze resonating knobs like an avant-garde hairdo, and it gave loud, slightly clanging notes with the *wah-wah* fluttering of overtones that guitarists call butterflies. From where I stood I had a short view of guavas, papayas, and rose apple trees, and a long view to the ocean on Maui.

We had a little cargo cult going in which we had learned how Zen Buddhism was done in a more or less Japanese way. In the original cargo cults, people in New Guinea saw airplanes landing and disgorging stuff—food, clothing, medicine, typewriters, Margaret Mead. So the New Guineans adopted a hunting metaphor; they cleared airstrips and built their own airplanes out of plywood and scrap. They were decoys to attract other airplanes with their cargo. In Hawaii, we were pretending to be Japanese to attract a change of heart. Black robes, incense, bowing, a Berlitz phrasebook of Japanese phrases. We had every kind of person, from Pulitzer Prize–winning poets and business types at the high end, tapering off into riff-raff—dope growers, psychotherapists, Australians—at the other end. We may have been riff-raff, but we were sincere riff-raff.

The teacher had a terrific story himself; he had been interned in Japan during the Second World War and learned about koans from the poet and translator R. H. Blyth. I'd gone to him for the excellent reason that he was the only person who answered letters from Australia. He hadn't had an enlightenment experience himself, he said, but he had a kind of cookbook from his teacher that allowed him to guide people through koans. The whole thing was best approached with a sense of humor, and the strange thing was that, for me, it was working.

My new thing was concentration. It wasn't a change of heart, yet it was something I could work on directly. It was like the fellow who lost his car keys in the dark alley but was looking for them under the streetlight. "There's more light here," he explained. I hoped that if I sat very, very still and didn't have thoughts, then lightning would strike. Tricky. Gradually things became clearer though. I would drive myself and, at the end of a retreat, fall into despair, having missed another opportunity to understand something beyond my small and miserable personality. Of course, it was my small and miserable personality that was in despair, too, and on good days I began to be amused by it. A grand Japanese teacher came to visit and I went in to see him, full of hope that somehow, perhaps now, indeed, why not now, if I were completely attentive, an experience would be triggered in me. He took one look at me, eager and overwrought, and patiently explained the beginning steps of meditation. "Just take this koan and keep it with you day and night . . ."

Then I went into a seven-day retreat for which I was well

prepared. While my friends went to the beach I stayed in at night and meditated. I thought I would be completely diligent and do the retreat without a moment's distraction. After a day or two, my mind was deep and clear, and then, suddenly, it wasn't. Wild and senseless thoughts zoomed by—images, songs, memories of earliest childhood, and memories I couldn't possibly have had. There was no pattern to my mind, and I could not begin to control my thoughts. I had done everything right and this was the result. I had failed. A tiny thought appeared, "Then this must be right." I just let my mind be whatever it wished to be, and immediately it calmed down. I had the sense of standing on the brink of a vast chasm and that I must have the courage to throw myself off. Yet I couldn't, I didn't know how. I was stuck there for a day or two, trying to overcome fear. Then I said to myself, "Okay, so you are afraid," and instantly the fear disappeared. Another tiny thought appeared, that I was the koan "No." I began to feel a connection to the universe. It seemed very funny that I had struggled so long to find a place in the universe when I couldn't fall out of the universe. It was as if a wave were struggling to understand what the sea was. I began laughing.

The teacher had a nice set of questions to test if you were really having some sort of profound experience. These questions, along with likely answers, had been handed down orally from Hakuin, an eighteenth-century Japanese teacher. I was very touched that Hakuin would have thought of this, thought of us across the centuries and oceans, and I found that the questions helped me find a language for my experience. They were odd but not random: questions such as "How high is *No*?" and "Explain *No* to a baby." The questions pushed me to see that a spiritual experience takes place in the life I actually live. So I laughed secretly to myself because life was so obviously tender and intimate. This laughter went on for months. The experience I had wasn't something to believe in; it was more a noticing, and a way of seeing. Also I found that I was at no risk of becoming saintly or of knowing all the answers. It was just that something in my heart was at rest and the world seemed a much kinder place. Other people seemed kinder than I and I was grateful to them for waiting for me to discover this. The world bubbled with light just under the surface, even when difficulties arose. I was beginning to love the whole of life.

It might be helpful to look at another, briefer, and recent account by a woman in northern California. She wasn't interested in meditation or in the Japanese aesthetic, but she was a pianist and the aspect of koans as art intrigued her. This is what she said:

> "No" was an incredible process for me. It took a year and a half. I kept a journal and had major dreams. Over and over again I came to my teacher and said, "It's this," or, "It's that." For a long time the teacher rejected my answers and this made me confident, since I didn't really believe them myself. "No" pushed other thoughts away. Familiar places looked like I had never seen them before. This happened in flashes at first, and then became more consistent. I found that I could survive frustration and the continual, tormenting "I don't know." I would sit and it would be "No" and in the afternoon, I was so tired and it was "No." In the evening there was a burst of energy and it was still "No." I got unhooked

from my condition; what was happening in my mind was just something happening in my mind.

I hit a dry place. "Why continue?" I thought. "I'm no good at this anyway. Why did I ever think that I could be included in this?" It was an important thing to go through the dry place, and it helped that I was encouraged to sit through it and value it. I realized that if I would just pay attention, little things would open up, little snatches. I was sorting seeds, as in the fairy tale. Being given a task, I thought, can be a form of grace.

Once, when I was also working with "No" in a retreat, I was with my son and a friend of his. I thought "Oh, I'll have to work at this. I'll have to be on as a parent." Yet when I went to look after the boys, I could see that they were perfectly right as they were and I just needed to be there and to enjoy them. They were running around and shouting and being perfect as boys. They really wanted me to hear their stories and when I felt their boy stories washing over me, it was another moment of thusness, like seeing sunlight falling across the wooden floor. Nothing was required of me. Before I'd had the feeling that when you see the thusness of things it is because you have become something special, but I could see now that it was just how things really are. The world came forward to me and it wasn't me going out to the world.

Then, in a retreat, we did walking meditation out into the parking lot. I said to myself, "This is a regal procession." I noticed the guy in front had a black silk shirt on; it had a dull finish. Redwood branches parted in front of my eyes and then there was that thing that's hard to describe, the nothingness, that wham of past, present, future gone—no separation between past and present. There is no self, absolutely none. The redwoods parted and it was whitish and granular, particulate, like seeing between the atoms. Who knows how long it lasted, but I found myself still walking when I arrived back, and my immediate thought was, "Wait, I have to be left with some word," and it was like, "Okay, if you insist on going back to this small world and having a word, even after everything has been shown to you, this is what you get: *No other.*"

Then I started getting really close to me: I would hold up my foot and say, "Here is *No* foot. How big is *No*? I am *No* size." The sense of kinship was very direct and obvious at that point. I would look at the wood floor and see that those cells are me. I would look at the rock and the rock was doing its rock thing. There is no separation, nothing in between the rock and me, nothing in between anything. Also, when I utter a word, I create the world. This came with the luscious sense that nothing has ever happened before. Also, of course, it all continues whether I'm mad or sad or get married or any of those things. Everything happens without needing me to do anything. The teacher, though, was still rejecting my answer.

Then "No" starts changing and I start to move on. It becomes a field of possibility. I hang out in this place for another six months. I don't need to own anything. I've already owned everything and been everything. The idea of a teacher confirming this seems totally ridiculous.

Later, still working with "No," I was at a retreat in the

redwoods again and walked into a first-floor bathroom. Though it was cleaned regularly, that bathroom always had the fragrance of pee. "No" became that whole fragrance and essence of pee. I wasn't drawn or repelled; there was just nothing else in the whole world. I didn't have to live with the fragrance of pee but did have to live with that discovery—no attraction, no repulsion, not doing, not picking and choosing. I used the tools at hand, in this case the pee. "What other tools," I thought, "would I use?" After that I could answer the teacher's questions, and the teacher finally passed me on "No."

Through the koans I stopped trying to improve myself. The koan had made me more interested in my actual life, and less interested in an ideal or spiritual life. There's a sense of staying with things, and of commitment as in my marriage, but at the same time there's not that fear of what would happen if something didn't work. I really don't care if we are in *this* house or have *that* TV. There are things I care about, but I can lose my arm and I'm still me. Can I lose that tablecloth? Yeah! And if I'm thinking something is not working, it's probably not working. When I rest in what I don't know, I stick up for myself.

For this woman, the moment of meeting the universe happened through meeting a part of it—a thought, a black silk shirt, redwood fronds, untangling a child's hair, the smell of urine, Blake's grain of sand. This raises a deep question. My own experience with the koan "No" didn't immediately change the shape of my life, though gradually it undermined the ramparts I had built against life. It was more that the koan reset my mind to zero.

Learning was easier since I lost my shame about not knowing already. Yet whatever I was incompetent at doing, I continued to have to learn, or not.

And here are some interesting questions I have been asking myself about the art in this koan: If an ordinary experience can be ecstatic, couldn't the moment a profound change of heart occurs be commonplace? Could that opening of the heart be going on all the time, unnoticed, a secret in plain sight? Couldn't it be something that is happening right now? Couldn't the home everyone is always looking for be right here, now? Could that openness be the natural state of the mind?

3

Rhinoceros

One day, Yanguan called to his assistant, "Bring me the rhinoceros fan."

The assistant said, "It is broken."

Yanguan said, "In that case, bring me the rhinoceros."

MEETING THE INCONCEIVABLE

Why, sometimes I've believed as many as
six impossible things before breakfast.

—THE RED QUEEN, RECORDED BY LEWIS CARROLL

WE SOMETIMES THINK of consciousness as a lamp, making a
golden cone of light on the surface of a desk. Outside the
yellow circle everything is dark and unknown. The usual way of
approaching things is to try to extend the yellow circle into the
darkness. Or perhaps to drag objects in from the dark. That is
working out of what you can conceive of, the bright area of what
you already know. This koan takes things the other way. Here you
depend on what is unknown and inconceivable to sustain you.
Most of life is inconceivable; even your left hand can't be fully
conceived of though it can be very useful. And if you try hard to
conceive of what your hand does, it won't play the piano very well.
The inconceivable is the source of all that comes into being. This
koan is not about making what is unknown, known. Instead it is an
exercise in relying on and making friends with the inconceivable,
using a casual event to start an exploration into the unlit realms.

The Koan

Rhinoceros

The Zen teacher Yanguan had an assistant who had walked in from the desert following the Silk Road. When he reached China, he took off his shoes and black sand fell out of them. At Yanguan's place he was given the job of making tea, taking messages, and waiting around until he was needed.

People came to Yanguan because they suffered and didn't know what else to do. The assistant was usually present when the teacher had public conversations, and he noticed that Yanguan had a knack of listening without putting distance between himself and the visitors. Soon the assistant, who had thought of himself merely as a witness, found himself being pulled into the stories he heard. He began to feel off balance a lot of the time. He felt even more off balance because with Yanguan he never knew whether he was in an ordinary conversation or not.

"All our conversations are ordinary," said Yanguan.

"Then why is it so hard for me to stay on my feet?" the assistant asked.

"No need to stay on your feet."

And there he was, off balance again. Strangely enough, this being off balance gave him hope and led him to stay with his teacher.

A traveler had given the governor a fan made of rhinoceros horn, and under the Zen rule that expensive, useless objects flow to those who don't care about them, the governor gave the fan to Yanguan. Everyone forgot about it, until one summer day, Yanguan asked, "Bring me the rhinoceros fan."

"The fan is broken," said the assistant.

"In that case," replied Yanguan, "bring me the rhinoceros."
The assistant was struck dumb.

Another of those present, Zifu, drew a circle and wrote the characters for the word *rhinoceros* inside it.

When Yanguan asked for the rhinoceros it was a world-stopping question for the assistant. The glue that connected one thought to another and that pair of thoughts to another pair and so on—the glue that made his reality—had failed. And this time, he didn't come back into balance. In his silence was a doubt that spread quickly to everything. Yanguan had told him that doubt is a valuable spiritual state, but he hadn't understood. Now he saw that this doubt was a form of spaciousness. It destroyed any trivial thought—almost any thought, actually. His rhinoceros was a doubt about everything he was. He couldn't be sure of his name, his purpose, even of the nature of a tree. He couldn't defend himself, he couldn't speak for himself since, at that moment, he wasn't a somebody to defend or speak for.

All of this happened in the blink of an eye. Yanguan had just asked for the rhinoceros, and Zifu, the other student, was drawing the characters. The assistant became entranced by the swirl of the brush, which seemed just right. It was a perfect gesture among many others—Yanguan's amusement, the jug on the floor.

Other moments and occasions fell into place for the assistant. He remembered times when he had heard the sound of a mallet, or seen geese flying in a lopsided V and somehow joined what he heard and saw. He had felt elevated and expanded for hours.

Once a visitor asked the old master, "What is the real body of the great Sun Buddha?"

The assistant groaned privately. Even he couldn't work out what the question meant, and it seemed to be far from the man's real life. The assistant was learning some things though: he saw that he was squirming because his own questions were like that too, designed to conceal his own helplessness and fear.

But Yanguan wasn't provoked by helplessness and fear and just said mildly, "Pass me that water pitcher."

The pitcher was in the new style—white with a blue fish—and had also been sent by the governor. The man brought it.

Yanguan then said, "Would you put it back where it was?"

The visitor did just that. He was eager to return to his important question, which he repeated. "What is the real body of the great Sun Buddha?"

"That old Buddha died a long time ago," said Yanguan.

The assistant began to laugh inwardly, not at the man but with him; he could see that the simple movement of the water jug held a beauty stronger than any religious idea. The laughter seemed to put him on the verge of a great discovery; then it subsided. The poor visitor had been so intent on his question that he missed the answer—a rhinoceros was in front of him, but he returned resolutely to the fan.

Years before, there had been a great persecution of Buddhism. The conflict split the royal family, and one night a prince came as a hunted man to Yanguan's temple. Yanguan asked no questions, took him in, and went one by one to everybody in the compound, even the children, with a simple message: "It's time to keep your mouth shut."

Everybody did—which made up another kind of silence in which worlds revolved. The prince stayed and stayed, finding that the interest in freedom which he had at first only feigned, turned out to be genuine. This discovery—that he was freer as a desperate fugitive than as a prince—was also the arrival of a rhinoceros.

When conditions were a little safer, Yanguan asked him to go back and be a prince again. The prince was reluctant. The force of this incident struck the assistant now; something precious was happening if the prince had to be persuaded to return to his previous life. The prince had given up the thought of being a ruler and then, under pressure, agreed to take up his throne again. The prince himself thought that his decision to return was stranger and more inconceivable than if he had decided not to return. Laughing, he embraced Yanguan, who was laughing too, and departed. These memories came back to the assistant in his silence, and we leave him there, motionless and full of life.

Working with the Koan

This koan points out that if you have a problem, you might not need to expand the pool of the known. Instead it might be possible to deal with problems that seem to be insoluble without translating them into something you can already understand. Taking such a course would mean accepting and even embracing being in the dark.

Here, you are simply presented with the inconceivable as though it were completely ordinary. If you are following along with Yanguan, you just say, "Okay then, if the fan is broken, sure, I'll get the rhinoceros." What is it that you thought you couldn't do and couldn't get? If your mind allows you to, perhaps you can just get the rhinoceros.

Can you remember a time when a situation stopped you in your tracks, not knowing what to do or say, your mind frozen by the rhinoceros of the apparently impossible, and while you stood there, another person simply acted and restored the flow of life? This koan can help you bring to life that other person within your self. Asked for a rhinoceros, Zifu immediately drew a circle and wrote in it the characters for the word *rhinoceros*. He was willing just to act even though a correct course of action was not visible before he began to move. If you are stuck in some way or in a tight corner and can't imagine a way out, this koan might help. It doesn't require you to know where you are going, or need a solution that makes sense in terms of the problem.

When something precious is damaged, almost everyone tries at first to mend it. For example, if you had had a terrible experience, or lost someone dear to you, you may think that you will not be able to survive or that you will never be happy again. It is easy to imagine that. However, if you rely on the inconceivable, you cannot know what will happen. What you can conceive of might take away your life. On the other hand, what you cannot conceive of might give you your life and even unexpected joy.

When a woman's child died, she immediately knew that it would now be impossible to witness tomorrow and everything past tomorrow—high school graduation, marriage, grandchildren. Conceiving of things has its uses, but in this case, everything she expected led to pain. It was as if she were trying to wish the fan back into wholeness, or to imagine a way to fix the broken fan. However hard she tried, it couldn't be restored. She found that she could only depend upon what was inconceivable.

When she accepted that her life was now outside anything she had ever imagined, there was no reason for living, and, at the same time, there was no reason why she couldn't survive or feel joy. Many people say things like, "My children give my life meaning," or, "My grandchildren give me a reason to live." This mother discovered, on the contrary, that the search for meaning led to unbearable sorrow. She had to live merely for the sake of life, without justifications or achievements. She found that she was willing to do this. It also came to her that taking this path was generous to her daughter.

She could think of her daughter with happiness, the way she used to wonder about her child's day in school. She could even speak with her child in her mind the way she did when she first knew she was pregnant. She did not have to think that her daughter's life was flawed or incomplete or that it came out wrong in the end. The perfection she had seen in her daughter as a baby extended to the girl's whole life, and even to her death. That was bringing the rhinoceros. Holding the thought of what should have or could have happened was trying to mend the broken fan. She was not who she had expected to be. In that way, she lived on and found a valuable life for herself. People often thought of her as kind and steady; she didn't think of herself at all. This too was bringing the rhinoceros.

Before the modern period, it was perhaps clearer that even an ordinary life can't be fully conceived. Major events often bore neither a signature nor a sensible explanation. People met plague, famine, and war and didn't have full information about what was going on. They might think that plague had something to do with rats or was related to an unfavorable conjunction of the stars, but they had no way to test their assumptions. The inconceivable nature of the world becomes obvious in times of catastrophe, yet it is always present.

We cannot fully conceive of the functioning even of common objects like a hand or a banana. The old teachers thought that what is inconceivable to us is, ultimately, the only thing that we can genuinely rely on. In this way they managed to find happiness inside disaster and peace inside war. When disaster is here, and you want to be happy, the happiness has to happen here, the dancing and the music here, even while there is disaster. Where else would you find happiness?

The inconceivable is present in the supermarket next to the cans of fajita sauce. All that is needed is for someone not to fulfill your expectations. For example, a stranger meets your eyes and you might look back without the thought that you are shopping and in a hurry. For that moment the world is composed of two unknown and equal beings. Then the next moment arrives with something different.

Everyone has seen kids in a parking lot doing a skateboard trick—not something spectacular—they just jump while the skateboard sticks to their feet. The only remarkable thing is that the way the board sticks to their feet looks impossible. They could never do this by conceiving of it, and they have no way of teaching it to one another. One kid does the trick and the others see it and try it over and over. They just rely on the rhinoceros.

Here is a slightly more unusual event in which something inconceivable happened. A friend was in the Paris Metro when a disheveled man came onto the subway train (I have heard a similar story from more than one friend, so perhaps it is an archetype of the Metro). The man seemed to be drunk or deeply disturbed; his shirt was off, he was bleeding, and perhaps he had been beaten up. He was sweating, gesturing violently, and swearing at the young women in the car. As he spoke, saliva sprayed from his mouth. It was clear, my friend said, that he wanted something, but he was also a frightening apparition and the young people in the car made themselves small and pressed back against the sides of the car, hoping not to be noticed. My friend, who is Japanese and already small, was not sure she understood what was happening, so she followed their cue and shrank back with them.

However, as the man stumbled along the aisle, an old woman, whom nobody had noticed until that time, reached up and took his hand. She tugged gently. His body followed her hand down, and he collapsed onto the seat beside her. As she held his head against her breast, he began sobbing. In this case the appearance of the rhino changed things for everybody in that subway car; a moment of fear and danger became an occasion for kindness. Such a transformation is one of the truly creative acts a person can bring about.

Science reconceives the nature of the physical world quite regularly, and lay people do their best to keep up by holding an appropriate mental image—perhaps by seeing the universe as a sort of giant orange, a fancy orange, with pips and odd swirls of galaxies. Buddhism also has its cosmologies. One teacher tried to get beyond the orange-with-pips model by building a room in which every surface was a mirror. The teacher and the emperor of the day entered the room in darkness, then a candle was lit in the middle of the room. The emperor was appropriately dazzled. It's nice to have your mind blown by a new concept, and dazzling ones are more fun. The rhinoceros koan, though, points to a way of functioning that welcomes any new conception of reality but does not depend upon it. Perhaps the excitement of a new idea comes partly from the feeling of freedom that accompanies the loss of the previous idea.

At the end, Yanguan, like everyone else, stepped into the inconceivable. When his time came, he just died peacefully, without much illness. The fugitive prince eventually became emperor, and returned to visit the training temple where so much had changed for him. But Yanguan had gone ahead, into death, and the prince didn't have a chance to thank him. Yanguan had often left a space where people were expecting something solid.

4

Ordinary Mind Is the Way

Zhaozhou asked Nanquan, "What is the Way?"
Nanquan said, "Ordinary mind is the Way."
"Should I turn toward it or not?"
"If you turn toward it you turn away from it."
Zhaozhou asked, "How can I know the Way if I
don't turn toward it?"
Nanquan said, "The Way is not about knowing
or not knowing. When you know something you are
deluded, and when you don't know, you are just
empty-headed. When you reach the Way beyond
doubt, it is as vast and infinite as space. You can't
say it's right or wrong." With these words, Zhaozhou
had sudden understanding.

THE HEAVEN THAT'S ALREADY HERE

Just watch children playing.
Eat vegetable soup instead of duck stew.

—MATSUO BASHO'S ADVICE TO POETS

IT IS NATURAL to look for the things you want outside of where you are now. That is the whole point of a journey. Yet this moment is all anyone has. So if freedom, love, beauty, grace, and whatever else is desirable are to appear, they must appear in a now. It would be nice if they appeared in the now you have now. And if they are to appear and endure they will have to be found in ordinary circumstances, since ordinary circumstances fill most of life. The marvelous, the lovely, will have to be right here in the room where someone is reading, someone is sick, someone is coughing, two people are making love, or a man is yelling at a dog. It will have to appear in the sound of rain splashing off trees, of a truck laboring up a grade, of TV from another room. It will have to appear in the sight of a child running, in the feeling of a headache, in the anxiety of preparing for exams, in worrying over a sick child, it will have to appear in what is ordinary, usual, commonplace, and right under your nose. Here is a koan about the heaven of the ordinary.

THE KOAN

Ordinary Mind Is the Way

From the age of eighteen Zhaozhou was the student of the great master Nanquan. He worked in the gardens, ran errands, studied, and tried to meditate, becoming half student, half son to the older man. The meditation was a problem. He wanted his meditation to be athletic, single-minded, convinced—everything he wasn't. He had a sense that there were great, spacious realms of consciousness, but not for him. As soon as he sat down to meditate, he wanted to get up again. He couldn't banish the flurry of distractions, or if he did, he just felt dull. So he asked for technical support.

Zhaozhou was unclear about the problem and so he was unsure what to ask. He was also embarrassed, so he began with a general question that didn't give too much away.

"What is the Way?"

"Ordinary mind is the Way," said his teacher.

"But that's just the problem," thought Zhaozhou, "I couldn't be more mundane. One minute it's all enlightenment this, enlightenment that, and the next I'm dreaming about girls." He couldn't imagine that the life he already had might be beautiful or true. He cut to his technical question.

"Should I turn toward it or not?"

"If you turn toward it you turn away from it." Nanquan seemed amused.

Zhaozhou considered this. The teacher had a point, but it was a very frustrating point. Sometimes the young man would think he was meditating, but he wasn't really; he was trying to meditate. The trying seemed to be in the way. It was like learning to swim: if you thrash about too much, you sink, but if you stop thrashing about, you float. Yet he had no trust in his body's buoyancy. "At first," he brooded, "you sink no matter what." And he was genuinely puzzled.

He had never done a single thing in his life without trying. His mind wandered. Recently he was having intense memories of childhood in which he seemed to be in his home, and to see the golden light coming through the door with such perfect richness that he might have bathed in it. But whatever came to mind, he thought, "This isn't it," and tried to push past it. Wherever he turned there was a wall.

He burst out, "How can I know the Way if I don't turn toward it?"

The teacher seemed to have moved closer, though in fact he hadn't stirred. The boy became calmer, aware of being close to the older man, of the scent of the pines, of the length of the moment, just as in his visions of childhood.

"The Way is not about knowing or not knowing. When you know something you are deluded, and when you don't know you are just empty-headed. When you reach the Way beyond doubt, it is as vast and infinite as space. You can't say it's right or wrong."

On the outside, these words didn't make any more sense than others Zhaozhou had heard, but at this moment he understood them. This completely surprised him and almost everyone else who knew him. It was not a great, crashing awakening, but still, it was a relief, something real to rest on. When he looked up, things were exactly so, the traffic on the road, the sound of a hammer—a genuine moment.

From that time on he was not in a hurry; he was happy with slowness and plainness—children growing, trees moving across a hillside, year by year. "Ah, this," he thought, "this, this." He never used energy that he didn't have to use. He studied with his teacher for forty more years until the old man died. At about sixty, he went on a long, slow pilgrimage for twenty years. He didn't bother teaching till he was about eighty and so old that it seemed somehow discourteous not to. It is said that he taught until he died at one hundred and nineteen. He was terrific at conveying the beauty of ordinariness.

WORKING WITH THE KOAN

When you observe common things closely they have an emphatic quality, a thusness that is like a charge around them and which is both beautiful and satisfying. To see the way the corners of the room meet or the light bounces off a floorboard is enough of a reason for life. Painters understand that the interesting object is the round glass, the box, the rusty down-pipe and that there is no need to reach for a meaning beyond what is visible. By their beauty, objects bring the eye of the beholder into contact with infinity.

There is another quality of ordinary mind, which is the interior of consciousness, the voices in the head, the shift of feeling and sensation. Yes, that's it, the voice in your head that says, "I don't have voices in my head." That one. Ordinary means that there is no need to add or take away from what is going on in the mind. Each portion of life has the whole of life. There is nothing wrong with what is in the mind except the sense that something is wrong. In this way simplicity turns to a form of compassion. When there is no objection to the states of mind that arise—ordinary or painful or thick—then they have their moment and move along, like clouds in the trade winds. And there is no flaw in the thinker or in the moment that is taking place.

Here is an ordinary-mind story about visiting a friend in a hospice. Like Zhaozhou, my friend was not in a hurry either. Usually one thinks of a hospice as something to do with dying and he was indeed dying, but on this day the story was simple and wasn't about dying at all; it was about men at lunch.

One morning I woke up and thought out of the blue, "Today is the right day to see Phil Whalen." I dropped my daughter off at school, got the blood test I get periodically, and drove down Highway 101 past sodden spring fields and through intermittent rain. Philip was a Beat poet and also abbot of Hartford Street Zen Center. At the time of this story he was in the San Francisco Zen Center Hospice on Page Street.

At first I can't get into the hospice, but I bang a lot and a well-dressed man in his late thirties pops his head out. He has the air of having come a very long way from an interesting room. "I'm not supposed to answer this door," he announces and disappears. By the time I get in, the only proof of his existence is that I am now standing inside instead of on the pavement. I wander around and go upstairs.

The rooms have gaunt, sleeping people in them. I find Philip's room because it is the only one with a closed door. Inside it is a world of its own. He is lying flat on his back staring at a ceiling he can't see because his diabetes has affected his eyes. He used to be rotund in the laughing-Buddha style. Now he is thin but not emaciated. He can't sit up without help. The classical music station KALW is playing something Mozarty with strings. There are daffodils in a vase and they make a yellow haze that he claims to see and appreciate. He tells me they are King Alfreds, he remembers these things.

"How are you, Phil?"

"Well, I'm not dead; it's most embarrassing."

"What do you think of, lying here during the day?"

"Well, I don't think. They call me up and ask me what I think—about reincarnation. I don't think anything about reincarnation. I think we should paint it yellow and stand it in a corner. And maybe dust it off every once in a while."

"And how does it go for you?"

"I get more irritable, but they don't seem to notice."

"Well, you've always claimed to be more obnoxious than others think you are."

"Hmmm. They're into process here."

"What do you mean 'process'?"

"How you are supposed to die."

"Hmmm."

"They want me to die in stages. I can't be bothered with that."

"Perhaps you could consider it a performance event."

"My hair is a mess."

Friends shave Philip's head for him, and he has something less than a centimeter of gray stubble on his head. He likes it smooth.

"So, I have to decide what to eat for lunch. Normally I would order Chinese, but it's hard to eat lying down."

"I could get you dim sum."

"But the dim sum factory is far from here and I think of dim sum as something you should eat while it's happening. Now someone brought me some good bread. I have a refrigerator under the bed and it's full of good things. It's a matter of deciding which good thing to put on the bread. Have you seen a tall, older man wandering around outside?"

"No."

"It's Carl. He is bringing me lunch."

"Well I'm here, I must be Carl today."

There is a refrigerator in a closet. It has salami, eight kinds of olives, Muenster. I raid the big fridge downstairs in the kitchen and also find a sharp Cheddar along with some raw onion. He sends me on a retsina hunt. He waves behind him at a pantry that I imagine existed in some other, perhaps now vanished, room. Spring sunlight angles through the window, frail and hopeful. Someone was supposed to bring a jar of retsina, and I search the room for it, but it is a small room and retsina is nowhere to be found. I crawl around for a while at eye level with the furniture legs. It is a pleasant thing to do and even becomes exhilarating. Crawling around on the floor is the best way of seeing a room, I decide. A bottle of Dos Equis turns up in the refrigerator and he declares, "That's it."

Philip eats slowly and appreciatively. Since he is blind, his hand reaches around thoughtfully as if it had an exploratory impulse of its own. It touches the pieces of food tenderly. The beer bottle he orients in this way: He lowers it gently and touches it first to his nose. Then he moves it carefully down his upper lip until he gets to his mouth and then he tips it and drinks. The sun, moving west, is warming and yellowing. At this time, he is not dying; I am not visiting a dying man. Two men are having lunch, one lying down, one sitting.

We talk books. He has Shakespeare to be read to him and

otherwise is fond of the eighteenth-century writers, has Gibbon's *Autobiography*, Boswell's *Life of Johnson*, Sterne's *Tristram Shandy*. I think then that he is an eighteenth-century man himself, with his large head that seems to be full of light, his detailed knowledge about so many things, his way of being spiritual but concrete. He has none of the misty romanticism that the Victorians passed down to modern meditators. And, unlike many Buddhists, he has not made a pretend Buddhist world to live in. He likes and dislikes this world with its physical pains and its pungent salami and the low, midday sun warming the window. He doesn't yearn toward another world than this one.

"I'm living too long, I may have to leave."

"How will that be, how is it here for you?"

"I like it here, they treat me well. But they are not allowed to give me certain drugs and so on, because I'm supposed to be dying more quickly. They may have to move me out, it's an administrative matter."

When I leave I kiss him on his stubbly head and shake his hand.

"I hope to see you again," he says.

Then he mumbles something. I wait a beat and turn back, "What was that?"

With the sweetest smile, he says, "Don't think it hasn't been real."

I could find nothing lacking or needing to be improved about Philip. There was nothing he needed to turn toward, no special way to go into the night.

After he died, I got a card about Philip's death. It mentioned his theory that he was a hospice failure and lived as long as he did because of a curse he had put on the grim reaper. A photo was included of Philip, making rings around his eyes with his fingers, as if he had found glasses that would allow him to see.

Ordinary mind is the Way.

5

A Condolence Call

Daowu and Jianyuan went to a house to offer con-
dolences. Jianyuan struck the coffin with his hand
and asked, "Alive or dead?"

Daowu said, "I'm not saying alive, I'm not saying
dead."

Jianyuan asked, "Why not?"

Daowu said, "I'm not saying! I'm not saying!"

On the way home, Jianyuan said, "Say something
right now, Teacher. If you don't, I'm going to hit
you."

Daowu said, "You can hit me, but even if you hit
me, I'm not saying." Jianyuan hit him.

After Daowu passed away, Jianyuan went to Shishuang and told him this story.

Shishuang said, "I'm not saying alive, I'm not saying dead."

Jianyuan asked, "Why not?"

Shishuang said, "I'm not saying! I'm not saying!"

At these words Jianyuan had an insight.

One day Jianyuan took a hoe, went into the teaching hall, and crossed from east to west and back again from west to east.

"What are you doing?" asked Shishuang.

Jianyuan said, "I'm searching for the sacred bones of our late teacher."

Shishuang said, "Waves flood every place, whitecaps overwhelm the sky. What sacred bones of our teacher are you looking for?"

Jianyuan said, "This is just what I need to strengthen me."

Fu of Taiyuan said, "The sacred bones of the late teacher are still here."

PURSUING DEATH INTO LIFE

I feel that my boat
has bumped, there at the bottom,
into something big.
And nothing happens!
Nothing . . . Quiet . . . Waves . . .
Nothing happens?
Or has everything happened,
and we are already at rest,
in something new?

—JUAN RAMÓN JIMÉNEZ

THERE ARE MOMENTS when you might discover with a shock
that what you know won't help you in the situation you are
facing now. A helicopter pilot told me he called this situation
"seeing the elephant," and for him it was a moment when winds,
cliffs, aircraft, and ocean made a situation that nothing in his
training taught him how to get through. Even so, without a plan,
he saved his aircraft and himself. Perhaps you have been stuck in
some way or just marking time, or doing everything perfectly

well—and then events have asked you to change something fundamental, perhaps your whole approach to life. Any occasion may provide the shock that begins such a journey. Brushing up against death, the prospect of which is well known to concentrate the mind, can often be that occasion. The point is that, in an impasse, life becomes more real and more interesting, so much so that it is better to have some impossible problems in your life than not to. In an impasse a risk is required; you have to give yourself completely to a new situation though you have no guarantees that your effort will turn out well. Here is a koan of such a shock and the journey that followed.

THE KOAN

A Condolence Call

The student's name was Jianyuan and his old teacher was Daowu. In those days people came to study Zen for many reasons. Some came because they were hungry, some because they didn't know what to do with their lives—the way others would join the army. Jianyuan came because he felt upside down and in pain. When someone congratulated him, he felt embarrassed. When he saw a lake full of clouds, its beauty didn't calm him; he became restless and wanted to talk. Everything he saw seemed at a distance. His mind was full of thoughts and feelings that put a curtain over the landscape. He wanted to break through that curtain but didn't know how. That's why he took the chance of studying with Daowu.

At the temple they meditated, worked in the garden together, studied. Life flowed along, and most of the time nothing much seemed to be happening. Occasionally Jianyuan would be visited by a vivid dream that stayed with him through the day. One such day, in the gardens, he felt that he was walking inside the body of Guanyin, the deity of compassion. He saw every leaf and little club of moss as a hand of kindness. Or at night, after meditating, he had a feeling of wholeness that he couldn't describe, and Daowu would just laugh when he made an attempt to do so.

These moments were beautiful but disappeared as quickly as they came, and more than anything, Jianyuan wanted understanding, a clear understanding that would open life to him. As the years passed, this unfulfilled desire became scarcely bearable. He began to take every opportunity he could to get away from the temple with his teacher. Quite often they walked to a nearby village to officiate at a funeral. The ritual for these occasions was well established: Daowu would offer incense, lead a chant, say a few words, and leave with his unobtrusive attendant. The bereaved families seemed to find this genuinely consoling.

On the day we are concerned with, everything appeared normal. Jianyuan noted the curved tiles on the eaves of the house as they entered. He took in the softly weeping wife of the man in the coffin, the son who was greeting the visitors, a couple of bright-eyed girls, the murmuring of friends and neighbors, their feeling of helplessness and goodwill.

Jianyuan became convinced that life would go on for this family and that their sorrow would pass, but he was no longer certain that his own life would go on. As usual, he walked toward the coffin to pay his respects, but his footsteps were heavy and slow, and when he saw the dead man his years of uncertainty became a weight in his chest. He began to feel unreal, to dread that he was not, himself, actually alive and that he would drift along in a kind of half-life until he just winked out of existence. He was no longer able to play the part he was supposed to play.

He raised his hand and smashed it down on the coffin, *Bang!* He turned to Daowu and, though he had not planned what he would say, a question burst out.

"Alive or dead?"

In the small room his voice was loud, but Daowu didn't show the least surprise and answered without hesitation.

"I'm not saying alive, I'm not saying dead."

Taking their cue from Daowu, the shocked mourners breathed out and returned to normalcy—tea and conversation. The young daughters were a little bit thrilled. They had heard of the strange behavior of people who were seeking enlightenment and now they saw it. But Jianyuan couldn't compose himself; his sense of the normal had shifted. He no longer knew whether his question applied to the corpse, or himself, or both, but it was the main thing in his mind, the most important thing of all, and he demanded to know why Daowu wouldn't help him.

"Why not?"

"I'm not saying! I'm not saying!"

Daowu was insistent, and Jianyuan managed to rejoin him in the ritual.

But some questions, once asked, cannot be unasked. On their silent walk home, the new moon in the rice fields, the silhouette of the chestnut were invisible to Jianyuan. He was helpless against his own doubt and the question it had raised. He couldn't stop asking himself, "Alive or dead?" As they approached the temple, Jianyuan grew more desperate. He began to feel that a possibility was slipping away and must be grasped. He became convinced that something was being hidden from him, and he planted himself in front of Daowu.

"Say something right now, Teacher. If you don't, I'm going to hit you."

Jianyuan was at the end of his tether; he shocked himself with this threat. Daowu wasn't shocked, though.

"You can hit me, but even if you do, I'm not saying."

Jianyuan hit him. Daowu picked himself up and walked on home. If anyone had been around, they would have seen an old man in embroidered abbot's robes bleeding slightly from a cut over his eye, humming to himself, and weaving ever so slightly, as if he were very tired or happy.

Jianyuan never returned to the temple. He didn't collect his books or his few belongings. There where he last saw Daowu, he risked everything, turned on his heel, and departed.

For years Jianyuan's question had a continuing life and gradually became so familiar to him that even when he was not consciously aware of it, it was present in a hidden way, like a seed or an underground river. The ears of summer grass whispered, "Alive or dead?" and the horse bending its neck to graze said, "I won't say! I won't say!" Time passed and the question remained. Frost was followed by plum blossom, new people were born and died, and he carried his question. After a few years, it might have been more true to say that his question carried him.

Then Daowu fell ill; his pain was visible and his students came to fuss over him. He said, "There is something which isn't repaid: Do you see that?"

Everyone wept, and then he died. When Jianyuan heard this story, he wept too. All sorts of thoughts appeared. The old man could have meant that his students hadn't repaid him, or that he, Daowu, had received something from the students and not repaid it. Jianyuan's mind started to spin just as if Daowu were with him again. He realized that he didn't have a clue what Daowu meant. He remembered that one repayment Daowu had wanted was for his students to understand, to awaken. Then Jianyuan did something he'd been thinking of doing for some time; he went to visit a teacher named Shishuang.

Shishuang had also studied with Daowu, and had his own story of wandering. At one time he stayed with the potters who lived at the edge of town, outside of the governor's protection and constraints. Everyone looked down on the potters, but Shishuang liked them. Perhaps he felt free there, where he could stretch out and breathe without anyone virtuous or important around, but Shishuang, like Daowu, didn't explain himself. Later he became a teacher, and his students meditated so much and sat so still that they were called "the dead tree gang."

Eventually, Jianyuan met with Shishuang. They sat together in the garden. His new teacher looked into his face with such directness that he immediately felt inclined to be happy.

He told Shishuang the whole story, starting with banging on the coffin. Before the tale was finished, Shishuang jumped into it himself and said, "I'm not saying alive, I'm not saying dead."

Jianyuan's doubt filled his chest again and he found it hard to breathe. Something was churning in him.

"Why not?" he mumbled.

"I'm not saying! I'm not saying!" said Shishuang.

At these familiar words, Jianyuan's thoughts stopped and his world stopped with them. Externally nothing changed. A light breeze shook the new leaves, the line of the hills was near on the spring day, and he noticed a garden mattock that needed to be put away. He hadn't gained any knowledge that he didn't have before.

But his mind was inexplicably buoyant and clear, as if he had stepped inside Daowu's mind. He was sure that he was meeting Daowu more deeply than he ever had in life. He saw Daowu's good-natured sense of humor. He had asked, "Alive or dead?" and now he saw the kindness of Daowu's reply, as though inviting Jianyuan to join him in freedom: "I won't say, I won't say."

"Today," he said to himself, "I have finally understood Daowu." Then he began to laugh at his own pomposity. He laughed at himself, he laughed at Shishuang, he laughed at the door and the floor. He tried the thought the other way round: "Today, with my happiness, I have misunderstood Daowu completely." And he laughed even harder. Shishuang walked outside with him, pointing out common objects—a bucket, the kitchen door. Jianyuan found everything amusing. Shishuang found Jianyuan amusing, or at any rate seemed to be enjoying himself too. Walking together in this way, the two men passed out of sight behind the great hall.

In time Jianyuan found that awakening wasn't only a piercing moment but something that seeped slowly through his life. Once he was sitting at evening after coming back from the gardens. Under a newish moon the crickets were getting a rhythm going, swallows were doing their last hunting. Dark came slowly so that he could still see the outline of the hills, like an afterimage from the day. He leaned on his hoe and remembered when he had traveled together with Daowu. He saw the lines on the old man's face, and the way he walked with a slight roll. Daowu's mind was so strongly present that, as if no time had passed, he was moved to continue the conversation that had begun all those years ago when he had banged on the coffin.

Jianyuan slung his hoe over his shoulder and went into the teaching hall, where he crossed from east to west and back again from west to east. People were coming in for an evening lecture, and they stopped in their tracks.

"What are you doing?" asked Shishuang.

His impulse was to help with whatever the project was.

"I'm searching for the sacred bones of our dead master," said Jianyuan.

Bringing his hoe to the teaching hall seemed a natural way to show what he had discovered. Those standing there laughed and, without being able to say why, felt themselves included in a delicious secret.

Shishuang said, "So? Waves flood every place there is, whitecaps are higher than the sky. What sacred bones of our master are you looking for?"

For Jianyuan, his teacher was enlarging what he had expressed.

"It's not only in the meditation hall—it's everywhere," he thought. "The sacred bones fill the universe."

Jianyuan had been looking at the hoe and had found it to be beautiful, the one thing that filled eternity. If he had thought about it, he would have acknowledged that it could have been anything, but for him, at that moment, it was a hoe. Shishuang had said, "Raise your eyes," and when Jianyuan did, everything he looked at shone. These fresh eyes, he thought, were what had been handed down from Daowu. A tired young man walked slowly past the hall and was also beautiful exactly as he was. The wall and the kitchen roof pierced his heart with their plainness.

"Thank you," said Jianyuan, "this is just what I need to give me strength."

The journey was becoming simpler. He felt that he was out walking with Shishuang in the cool of the evening, and that they had just come up with Daowu and resumed an old conversation where they had left off.

A teacher called Fu of Taiyuan heard about Jianyuan striding into the hall with a hoe. He too jumped into the story and said, "The sacred bones of the old master are still here." In this way the story was remembered and passed around among the fellowship of those who ask questions about what matters. For the rest of his life Jianyuan kept walking with such companions, though to an observer it might have seemed that he was often alone.

WORKING WITH THE KOAN

In this koan, the teacher helps the student by refusing to give the kind of help he is being asked for. This refusal is an example of what psychologists call holding a container for change, and the teacher got clobbered for it, which you will probably think is only fair if anyone has ever helped you in such a manner. The teacher's not saying, though, turns out to be a tool for the student to get through the impasse, surprising everyone. The ancient way of working with the koan is to carry the question with you wherever you go.

So, your life goes, getting up (Alive or dead?), drinking coffee (Alive or dead?), driving to work (Alive or dead?), watching a movie (Alive or dead?). You can also carry the teacher's response, "I'm not saying! I'm not saying!" discovering what you lose when you do say, and the invitation in "I won't say, I won't say."

Working in this way loosens the knots in the mind, and it also introduces a space so that you can start moving between anxieties and distractions and not struggle with them so much. Just staying with the questions, life grows calmer and more interesting. If this koan has chosen you, or called to you, it naturally belongs with certain other questions, deep questions, which then become yours. What happens to me when I die? What happens to me when those I love die? When someone has died are they alive in my mind or dead? In what way are they still alive and in what way not? And of those people who are still alive, are they really alive in my mind or are they dead?

After the death of my mother I noticed that I didn't have a repertoire of off-the-shelf feelings. Sometimes I was sad, but mostly I was happy in a way unconnected to her going. Sometimes I was forgetful. When I poured her ashes off an old cast-iron bridge into the river she had lived on all her life, it seemed an intimate and friendly act, and I felt close to her in ways I sometimes had not in life. She was still alive in me, and I had confidence that we would both, in our separate times and ways, find the sea.

Without off-the-shelf feelings, or off-the shelf-thoughts, we are not so sure of what is alive or what is dead. A bachelor friend married a woman with children and told me:

> I had killed off the possibility of deep interaction with children. I had closed off that possibility without understanding what children could bring. I had a narrow sense of what my path was. But that's exactly what you learn — that if you approach small children without an agenda, if you can match the openness of their minds, you too are open. My wife's little boy just comes to see me and doesn't know why, doesn't have the slightest idea of what should or shouldn't happen. If I avoid structuring things in my usual way, I meet him in the same way he meets

me. Then his older brother got interested in the Beatles and wanted to learn guitar. So I resurrected something from years ago when I played guitar for a while. I had put it away, assumed it was dead. And perhaps he'll continue with guitar or not, but I think I will anyway.

And what do you presume to be alive that might be dead? Work, even good work, can become soulless; some friendships grow rote. And sometimes, wondrously, you might find that an old wound, a sorrow you have carried very carefully like a glass filled to the top with water, has no longer any life or interest in it and does not require you to keep a watchful balance anymore.

Then there is a family of questions about not saying: Why is it sometimes better not to say? Is there a kind of saying that makes the world retreat from us? It is possible to start talking too soon at the end of a disturbing movie—to reassemble the world by analyzing the movie, or by talking about something else. A professor showed a classic movie to his class every week and left time for discussion afterward. One week's film left the students in silence. When the lights came up and the discussion period began, half the class got up and left the room. The movie was still alive inside them, and they wanted to keep it that way.

In ancient times there were mysteries celebrated in Eleusis. The initiates were forbidden to speak of what they underwent, and though the tradition lasted for more than a thousand years, we still do not know what happened there. Perhaps the secret was kept because the procedures of the initiation weren't in themselves so mysterious and the effects on the initiates couldn't be understood from a description of the outer events.

One of the strangest ceremonies I have ever participated in

occurred when a group of men in retreat dug a hole in the ground and took turns going to whisper into the earth every sorrow or shame that burdened them. It was a way of saying and of not saying at the same time. It seemed to help; the action gave me a sense of the welcoming quality of the earth and the common fate of humanity as other men in the darkness nearby whispered their own griefs. Keeping silent may not mean that nothing is being acknowledged; it may mean that something is valuable but can't be illuminated by light and understanding and needs darkness to come to resolution. In folk tales, keeping silent may break a spell or allow time to pass so that growth can occur.

Daowu encourages the work in the night to go on by bringing Jianyuan's impasse into awareness without resolving it. He says, "I'm not saying! I'm not saying!" and in his kindness he takes a difficult question and makes it worse. Perhaps it is when you meet a real impasse that the true purpose of your life begins to unfold and your true journey begins. Jianyuan's virtue was that he didn't refuse the journey. This koan has always encouraged me to trust the difficulties I run up against and the slowness with which I work with them. It is as if an impasse has its own journey built into it, a journey that belongs only to that impasse and which is a unique path to freedom.

Each step in the dark turns out in the end to have been on course after all.

6

The Red Thread

Songyuan asked,
    "Why can't clear-eyed Bodhisattvas sever the red thread?"

CONNECTIONS THAT DESIRE MAKES

Friday I tasted life. It was a vast morsel.
A Circus passed the house—still I feel the red
in my mind though the drums are out. The Lawn is full of
south and the odors tangle, and I hear today for the first
time the river in the tree.

—Emily Dickinson

We must agree on what matters: kissing in public places,
bacon sandwiches, disagreement, cutting-edge fashion,
literature, generosity, water, a more equitable distribution of
the world's resources, movies, music, freedom of thought,
beauty, love.

—Salman Rushdie

DESIRE BURNS at the core of life, and it's usually complicated.
"If you love me then I don't love you," as Carmen sings. One
spiritual solution to desire is to flee it. The idea is nonattachment,
transcending the body and its feelings—an intellectual form of

taking a cold shower. But trying not to think about what you want sets up an inner conflict and is not the same as freedom. Desire might be handled in another way, as a given. What you want is a portion of the world rising out of nothingness to meet you. It has its own purity just by existing. It is as real as the Sydney Opera House or a wombat. You can't transcend a wombat. Perhaps desire is necessary for life and fundamental to empathy. You might find freedom by going toward the disturbing force rather than away from it. There is nowhere outside the body you can live, so you might find freedom in the body. One koan about desire consists of a simple question.

The Koan

The Red Thread

Songyuan asked,
    "Why can't clear-eyed Bodhisattvas sever the red thread?"

Working with the Koan

The idea here is that a red theme runs through everyone's life. This red thread is passion and sorrow—all the vulnerability and desire that link you to the world. The direction this thread takes in your life is only gradually observable over time. It is the color of blood, of fire, of sex, of intimacy. To connect, to help, to be of use in this world, you have to walk with people. You have to let them act upon you also, and you won't remain unchanged. The interesting thing here is that the person who is attached to desire is the one who is a Bodhisattva, the Buddhist version of a saint who is seeking to help others. Your own desire, your own red thread, might be the source of your empathy for others. Song-yuan, who made this koan, was explicit about this. Sometimes he said, "It's the red thread between your legs."

In this koan there is also a sense that love is the enemy of purity. Mohammed Atta, whose fanaticism led him to pilot one of the airplanes into the World Trade Center, found the presence of women polluting, and it makes sense that someone who would commit random killings for the sake of an idea wouldn't enjoy life very much. Puritanism takes many forms—counting the worth of people only as numbers, which the corporate and bureaucratic mind loves to do, is puritan because it ignores the necessary uniqueness of each person. Also, when religious parents don't want children to be taught evolution, there is a puritan fear of being part of the natural world, of losing oneself in nature and desire. During the time of the airplane attacks that destroyed the World Trade Center, John Ashcroft, attorney general of the United States, used to give press conferences in front of a bare-breasted statue of Justice. It evidently embarrassed him to be talking to television audiences with a half-naked woman standing behind him, so he arranged for curtains to cover her when he spoke. Hmmm. Justice without breasts is a bad sign for mercy.

The red thread is always tangled and resists the simplification of life into formulae. No matter how pure you are, you might change your mind, fall in love, or forget to punish someone. Erotic connections turn life upside down, and when life is too tight, turning things upside down can be a good thing. This koan resists the totalitarian impulse in spiritual paths.

I knew a man whose life had a great deal of the red thread in it, and who was also a Bodhisattva of sorts. There is more than one kind of darkness in his story, and some might think it did not end well, yet for me, it is about the shapes love takes.

Tommy Dorsey was a performing drag queen who discovered an enthusiasm for Zen Buddhism, an enthusiasm that, for some years at least, saved his life. He became a priest, shaved his head, was given the name Issan and wore the formal kimono-like robes that went with the role in Japan. "I still wear a skirt, but I gave up the heels," he said. His dedication surprised many people, and when his teacher made him the abbot of a small Zen center in the Castro District in San Francisco, it was a big event. The Castro was a place for the gay revolution with its arts, its parties, its style, and its joie de vivre, and Issan was part of these happenings. Then, in the early 1980s, AIDS started to appear and at first no one knew what to make of it. Whatever the disease was, there were very sick young men who were in the streets with nowhere to go.

There was a medieval echo in this plague because it was little understood and because it was often disfiguring. There were people who shunned the sick men—"I'm not letting you eat off my dishes; you'll infect my kids"—and there were hands that reached out to catch the falling bodies and asked for nothing in return. In northern California, lesbians were prominent in the caretaking movement, and there was a sorrowful repetition of the old motif of the woman holding the body of a young man. It was nursing time and funeral time. It was red thread time, when desire and kindness and death were intimately twined together, and the puritans had very little to contribute.

One day, Issan brought home with him a man who had become too sick for his roommate to manage. The man was called JD and seemed to be going down fast. Issan thought that he and his friends at the Zen Center (whom he consulted beforehand, though without really explaining how much everyone's life was about to change) would take care of JD until JD died.

Issan didn't think of anything he did as noble or good—being good in conventional ways wasn't his strong suit anyway—and this more or less involuntary act of kindness seems to me deeper than a thought-out choice might be. He knew a lot about desire and love, and this decision came over him the way desire would. It was a red-thread moment and also a moment of simple fellow feeling. Issan's thought was that JD would get a good, dignified death in a few weeks, and, after he was gone, Issan intended to haul someone else home.

But JD had other ideas. He became delirious and paranoid, manifested many terrifying symptoms, and then revived. He wangled himself a motorized wheelchair in which he hotrodded around the Castro. He took this chariot by BART, which is the Bay Area's Rapid Transit system, to Oakland and came back with an iguana. He demanded martinis. He eventually traveled to Florida to say goodbye to his family. JD smuggled his pet onto the plane and somehow lost him there, after which he locked himself in the bathroom at thirty thousand feet. And in Florida, eventually, he died. This is another thing about the red thread: if you help people, they will be unpredictable and do inconvenient and, possibly, dangerous things. When you take in a person with AIDS, dementia might be a factor on top of tuberculosis and shingles and other, stranger diseases, yet even so, beauty might be linking everyone concerned.

Issan's fate was interlaced with others like JD. Being Issan meant being tangled up with the consolations and transgressions of desire—he carried that power and that blessing. He had a lover whom Phil Whalen called Sweet Baby James, but not to Issan's face. Issan had known James for years and considered him one of his transcendental experiences. James was a street kid who could indeed be charming and then again could go crazy and roller-skate around the zendo and threaten people. Issan thought he must have caught AIDS during a weekend involving "James, a cheap motel, and a bottle of cheap gin—no, no, it was a bottle of good gin, actually. I can't stand the cheap stuff." This was the sort of adventure that had something dark and unconscious about it and that nevertheless was also threaded through with what was exciting and sympathetic about Issan.

It is not necessary for desire to kill you. Issan was killed by cir-cumstances and luck, not desire. He was like someone who is in a market, picking up a bottle of wine, when it is bombed. You could say that the desire for wine killed that person, but if she had been out buying bread, would you say that she was killed by her desire for bread? You need courage to find out what you really want in life, and what you want might be dangerous. But life is dangerous anyway, and there is a beauty in becoming more and more fully who you are, in paying attention to, as well as being pulled along by, your red thread. For me, the story of Issan's life is not just about sex. The red-thread quality lay in his being emphatically who he was, and how he brought that sexy drag-queen quality of his to looking after people. The red thread was most visible in that moment of picking people up off the street and finding a home for those who had none.

Issan seemed to contemplate his own demise very little; it was just present and looming. This did not seem to be denial. He would complain: "Oh it hurts! It's too cold. They never get the pleats right. The garlic is very strong, don't you think?" and there was something dramatic and endearing about it. He complained about real things, yet not about his fate. Issan proved an exception to Montaigne's rule that no one is a hero to his servants: those close to him found him happy and loving, though inclined to turn their lives upside down.

My favorite story of his dying is this: Toward the end, Issan needed assistance walking and a friend was helping him back from the bathroom. They paused on the first-floor landing. The friend, a person himself so fiercely nonconformist that he was nicknamed "the feral monk," was overwhelmed by feeling, a previously un-heard-of event. He took a deep breath and said, "I'll miss you, Issan." Issan turned his large, liquid, seductive eyes on his friend and said, "I'll miss you too. Where are you going?"

Kindness and wildness is a poignant combination. It is without premeditation and does not ask for our good opinion or seek pay-ment for good deeds. Maitri, the AIDS hospice Issan founded, became an institution, which grew and helped many. There are people who think Issan was a saint, and even people who think that after his death he interceded for them in heaven and cured them of AIDS by his blessing. I think he would have enjoyed that, the way he might have enjoyed someone finding the face of Lana Turner on a tortilla. The more interesting point for me is the one about the red thread—that everyone has some sainthood pos-sible, and that the unfolding of their goodness might sometimes be through their transgressions, through what is wild and imper-fect in them. Issan seems never for an instant to have thought of his life or his death as a tragedy. The point of this koan might be found in truly living your life rather than living it perfectly or even respectably.

Eventually Issan died in his temple. He died before JD, the patient he had first brought in. I sat with his body one night after his death. He was laid out in a white kimono—white for death. The windows were open to cool the room and the white curtains flapped and sighed. Every now and then I would think he spoke and begin to ask, "Say again, Issan?" and then realize that, no, it was just very quiet. He and I were both very quiet. Then friends came in and embraced him and stroked his cold cheek and wept and spoke to him as if he were alive. Someone had told him that they thought AIDS terribly unfair.

"You get what you deserve," he replied, "whether you deserve it or not."

7

Counting the Stars

Count the stars in the sky.

A BORING KOAN

Lower your standards.

—WILLIAM STAFFORD'S ADVICE TO POETS

Never think of yourself
as a person who didn't count—
Festival of the Souls.

—MATSUO BASHO'S POEM ON THE DEATH
OF HIS FRIEND, JUTEI, IN JULY 1694, NEAR THE
TIME OF THE JAPANESE ALL SOULS' DAY

THERE ARE PASSAGES in life that seem as if they are between other passages. There may be nothing wrong with them, but they don't have much heft of their own. Such moments are vestibules or airport lounges; you pass through them not for their own sake but in order to get to other moments. The range of these *between moments* or intervals can be wide. Times of physical pain often take such a form, as can waiting in line for a driver's license, and in general waiting for someone else to do something—

for example, to sign a deal, to grant you a visa, to die, to fall in love with you, to be impressed by you, or to pass sentence on you. One of the virtues of meditation is that it allows you to tolerate or even enjoy such between moments, to befriend the material your mind throws to the surface when it is not otherwise occupied by chasing something or trying to improve its condition. There is a koan that encouraged me to examine such moments.

THE KOAN

Counting the Stars
Count the stars in the sky.

WORKING WITH THE KOAN

For a long time, this koan lacked interest for me, was possibly downright boring. The koan is usually given to someone soon after their heart has started to open up. At that moment you might feel as if you are floating on the ceiling. It is said in the koan schools that, if you awaken in the morning, you don't mind dying that evening, your life has been worth it. You can see your place of belonging, how you have a home in the oak tree and your neighbor and the elk rubbing its velvety antlers on a gray fence post. In this razzle-dazzle, you might forget that you are also yourself, Sally or Bill. This koan seemed to remedy that tendency, by insisting on the mundane and particular. Counting, numbering, taxes, deductions, interest rates. The koan doesn't allow you to be vague and enthusiastic the way spiritual expressions can sometimes be. It asks for embodiment and precision.

The traditional response that has been passed down is just to count the stars. That's fun, because it's impossible, though not wildly so, since the activity of counting is a familiar one. I had noticed, along with the other teachers I worked with, that no one had ever had much to say about counting the stars. "This could be interesting," I thought. "What if I have found a boring koan? Perhaps I should feature it in some way: BORING KOANS AVAILABLE HERE." No one's heart seemed to be changing, and though that might be the point of a boring koan, for me this koan was like an apple tree that had always been in the garden but had never flowered.

Some passages in life seem plain or nondescript, yet they might make life sing, the way an anonymous brown bird hopping under the orange tree makes the garden more alive. Some people fight boredom in meditation, yet to be bored can be a good thing; it can mean the beginning of an appreciation for bare, plain qualities. Enduring your own consciousness is so valuable, I thought, Why shouldn't a koan be there just to bore you? In this way, might not you appreciate your mind even when it is not being amused or having a problem?

Intervals, and moments between other moments, can be good. In airport gates and shops and bars, you enter a boring eternity which can sometimes be soothing. I think airplane crashes, so infrequent compared to car wrecks, are especially shocking because the point of being in an airliner is that nothing happens. Like an elevator, it's a place of boredom, not of events. The Tibetans have the word *bardo*, which is often applied to the imagined realm you travel through after death. *Bardo* means "between," and all human states are actually bardos: Waking is a between state, and dreaming while you sleep is a between. Dying is its own between, and death, when in that imagined life you wander until a rebirth seizes you, is also a between state. Life is understood as intervals between other intervals. So far, so good.

Now when you are working with a koan, it's most interesting if you consider that everything going on for you is connected to that koan. Everything you think and feel, every reaction you have to events, is in the field of the koan, the way the earth is in the gravitational field of the sun.

Also, when you are in the field of a koan you usually notice two opposite experiences. One is a sense of the vast background, the eternity that is inside everything you do and through which you move each day. From this point of view, life is not a mistake, and there is no in-between moment that has less value than another. The beauty of common things shocks you, there is nothing boring about them. It is this experience that people talk about when they speak of enlightenment, or intimacy, or a profound change of heart. It's a happy moment.

I have noticed that a koan usually has a quite different and darker effect as well. This other effect of a koan is to evoke, how to put it? . . . the delusion, the belief system, that seems to belong with this particular koan. This belief system is an assemblage of painful thoughts. It might seem as if you are failing. You might say to yourself, "This is way too hard," or "I'm an idiot," or you might suddenly remember old grievances as if they had just occurred. These painful thoughts don't mean that you are failing. Instead, they mean that this is how pain appears to you, this is the aspect of your imprisonment that this koan evokes. For example, any koan that depends on a comparison can evoke a fierce feeling of superiority or humiliation. The koan "The great way is not difficult, it just avoids picking and choosing" might bring up lots of picking and choosing and all the hope of gain and fear of loss you have ever had. Such a koan can show you everything you don't like about your own consciousness when you pick and choose. It can also be true that if a koan makes you suffer in such a way, then it might be especially useful to you. And if you are interested in freedom, it might lie in this direction. You could go toward rather than away from the sign in your mind that says NO TRESPASSING.

And what does finding freedom mean? When you are objecting to the moment, you are treating the moment as a between, a faux moment, a mistake, not a real moment to be inhabited. If you see that your thoughts are the source of your pain, freedom begins. You have been a character in a novel and suddenly you stop following the script and step out of the novel. No extra effort is needed; you don't need to write a better script. At the moment of his awakening Buddha said, "I have met the builder and broken the ridgepole. I shall not build that house again."

For me, the delusion that came with "Count the stars in the sky" was that it was boring. Then one evening an engineer told me how he had been touched by it, and I understood the koan the way he did. First of all, he had a dream about koans generally. He dreamed of a complicated lock, with moving parts. When you aligned them just right, you could see the moon through the keyhole. The lock was antiquated, and he was working out how to deal with it. That was a promising set of images—of koans as antique locks and also as windows into a moonlit world. When he woke, he felt encouraged. One night he went out onto the verandah and there was fog in the redwoods, wrapped around the great trunks. The next night was clear. He started, "One, two, three . . ."

He enjoyed the counting. There was nothing down to earth about it. The vastness of the galaxy was in each star. There were too many stars to count, and yet the count went on like a prayer. The next day he kept repeating to himself, "Count the stars in the sky." As he drove and ate and talked to his family, he kept the koan with him. He noticed that, when he was with the koan, little things—being short of sleep, the market taking a dive, feeling a physical illness—didn't throw him. He kept counting. He counted some more stars and asked himself, "What is counting the stars?" The next day was intense at work and he forgot the koan for long stretches, but when he got in the car there it was. It was as if the koan began to hold the koan. The next day, every situation had an illumination of its own. The color of leaves was intense. He was full of joy. The next day, when he saw the plainness of objects and people, he wasn't happy or unhappy. He wasn't moved to speak about this plainness. He saw that this was the traditional response to this koan; that counting was itself a complete thing. He continued with the koan.

Then he came to talk to me. He jumped up, opened the door, and pointed out to the redwood trees and Douglas fir, the early evening sky darkening among them, the rough rock wall, the moss and trillium, and the fall away into the valley. He was excited, he felt so befriended by life, and so unafraid. He pointed to himself and to me and to the lamp.

"That's a star, that's a star." He pointed to a table. "That's a star." He pointed to a flower arrangement. "That's a star." He pointed to himself. "A star."

"What about terrorists?"

Yes, terrorists too. Definitely stars. He pointed through the window again to the evening. "There is no death because all this is me. All of these stars."

We sat together in the silence, then talked for a while, then I gave him the next koan and he left.

Then I began to remember. I remembered Mr. Roland, a retired gentleman in a brown suit, to whom I had just introduced myself, who taught me to count to one thousand at the age of four. We were standing beside snapdragons at his front gate. I remembered my grandfather teaching me the names of stars, constellations, galaxies—Canopus, in the great ship *Argo;* the Crow; the Magellanic Clouds; Orion with his sword and his red shoulder; the giant star Betelgeuse, a hunter accompanied by his dogs, chasing the Pleiades. He taught me how some names were from Arabic because of the desert astronomers: Aldebaran, the eye of the Bull. Some Aborigines called the Southern Cross the Swan. My grandfather also brought out his antique sextant—teak, ivory, brass, and smoky-colored glass you looked through. Standing beside me on the black street above the chimneys of the public hospital, he taught me how to find my latitude, just in case. He told me it was worth your while to know the names of the stars, to be able to navigate by them, and to contemplate vastness. Pacing the bridge of a ship on watch at night is good for this activity, he advised.

I saw then that this is one of those embarrassing stories in which the storyteller unconsciously describes his own mind. I thought the koan was boring, but I hadn't let it all the way in. I thought the koan was lazy, but no, that was also me. And I had convinced a few of my colleagues as well. It's really nice to have your delusions exploded; it's like getting out of prison. If you can see a delusion of your own, it's wonderful, you can breathe, you

can't find the walls that lately hemmed you in. I like to sit on a verandah overlooking the valley, counting the Pleiades coming up in
the cold air, the Crow, the Big Bear turning around the pole as the
night goes on.

And that's what meditation is like really, doing nothing, looking at nothing in particular, relishing the plainness, the life in
between.

8

Out of Nowhere, the Mind Comes Forth

The Diamond Sutra says,
"Out of nowhere, the mind comes forth."

LIGHT PLAYING ON
CHILDREN'S FACES

You tell me you're innocent
and you're clutching the loot.

—WUMEN HUIKAI

Spring rain—
the girl is teaching the cat
to dance.

—KOBAYASHI ISSA

TIME ORGANIZES ITSELF INTO JOURNEYS. The standard
idea of how to fall into a profound change of heart involves
seeking knowledge afar. Yet if wisdom comes out of nothing, the
way the big bang, and hydrogen, and gravity, and space-time did,
then it is possible that the standard idea is not true. Going on a
journey depends on the assumption that something is lacking at
home. It can seem so obvious that something is lacking now that

most people never check. Yet such an idea could itself be a fiction. What if you did check and found that nothing was wrong? Then you might go on a journey just for fun. And children, before they are taught to go on their own long journey, might understand that whatever part of life they have is complete.

The Koan

The Diamond Sutra says,
"Out of nowhere, the mind comes forth."

Working with the Koan

Usually people work hard to make things happen. Yet it might be that things happen by themselves, coming out of nowhere. Here's a story about understanding coming out of nowhere for a child in kindergarten.

Some of the old school buildings in Los Angeles had high ceilings and clerestory windows. A boy was sitting at his little chair in kindergarten when he saw the yellow light coming in through the high windows. Dust motes swirled in the beam of light. He noticed how bright they were and kept watching; then, suddenly there was no distance between him and the light. He disappeared. He didn't know how long he was gone; there was no time. When he heard a voice calling, he didn't recognize the name at first; it didn't have anything to do with him. Then he heard the other children laughing and wondered what they were laughing about. It was the teacher calling him. After that, the things he saw were beautiful in themselves. Faces seemed more real, and what was real was beautiful. He didn't really have a name anymore; he was the beam of light. And it didn't have to be a beam of light. It could be a Coke can or another child, and he would feel that connection. His sense of yours and mine had shifted to something like, "My hamburger is yours, your house is mine." When the grownups around him fought and argued, he felt sad for them, that they didn't understand, and couldn't see what he could see.

My own experience of being a child was that we were little monsters—fighting, stealing, boasting, lying, and tricking each other—and at the same time, the trees above us and the afternoon blessed our shouts and the gravel in our knees. We took life for granted because we knew something important. Here is my story about what children know. I was three or four and used to play in the gutter outside my grandparents' house, where my family lived. This was mildly, though gratifyingly, offensive to certain adults, who muttered things like *guttersnipe* when they had to walk around my mud pies. Once I was playing with a couple of new trucks, so it was after Christmas, and I was with Robert, a boy a little older. He told me how robbers had broken into his house the night before and stolen his toys. His parents were apparently helpless in the matter. "What a stroke of luck," I thought, "that I have these new toys, just at this time." So I gave them to him.

At that time, my parents were fairly poor, and I only had about four toys, so they noticed, and asked after my trucks. When I told them about the robbers and my good luck, I saw the geometry of their faces rearranging itself. In a flash, my understanding rearranged itself too, and I realized that there might be hidden corridors in the other boy's problem with robbers. The interesting thing is that I then felt sad that he thought he needed a truck to be happy. Trucks were good for playing with friends or for giving away. That was obviously their only purpose. Children see this communion of all beings—until they arrange themselves more tightly, and then they don't.

The child's mind is not free because it's a child's mind; it's just free because it's free. Here is another example of the free mind at work. Usually, people think of death as very important and gruesome. Yet if you are identified with the background, the inconceivable nowhere that the foreground came out of, death might not be a terribly significant event. It might not mean what you expect it to mean. When her mother was dying, a friend took her young son back to his grandmother's home. The grandmother had a special bed with a railing around it. The boy couldn't walk yet but would cruise along using tables and the bed railing to hold himself up as he went. The two women watched him. He looked very cute, which was their word for thusness. The dying woman said, "Oh, I'll always remember that."

If children can have a natural clarity, you might too, even if you remember no operatic enlightenment experience. There might be no good reason for this clarity; it could be something that just is the case, like a tree, like life. All you would need to do is to notice that things are clear, or to throw overboard the idea that things are not already clear. You could find that courses of action appear to you out of nowhere just the way the next moment does. Your navigation could unfold by itself, and the universe might provide the beauty and happiness you seek.

When you forget your carefully assembled fiction of who you are, you can find a natural delight in people, in the planet, the stones, and the trees. There is no observable limit to this beauty, and no one is excluded from it. Then, if you are fighting an enemy, you may be fighting them as well as you can, but you won't be a true believer. You will know that an enemy is not truly other and that the fighting is some kind of misunderstanding. The worries that lead to quarrels may still be present, but they are not the main thing. Your problems could be a kind of dream, very powerful when you are in it, and yet a dream. You might notice that, even deep in dreaming, you are near to waking up. And the more you are awake, the kinder the world might seem.

9

Tortoise Mountain Wakes Up

Yantou and Xuefeng were snowed in on Tortoise Mountain. Day after day, Yantou slept while Xuefeng sat up and meditated.

On the third day, Yantou sat up too and said, "Get some sleep. What do you think you are—a roadside shrine?"

Xuefeng touched his chest and said, "My heart isn't at peace. I can't fool myself."

Yantou gave a great yell. "Don't you know that the family treasure doesn't come in through the gate?" he said. "Let the teaching flow out from your own breast to cover the sky and the earth."

Xuefeng was suddenly enlightened and cried out, "Today Tortoise Mountain has finally awakened!"

FRIENDSHIP

We'll walk above the vineyards,
whisper together—
laughing, the tendrils uncurling,
sky bending, a dry earth beneath;
sun stripes on hillflank,
heads leaning together
and never tire of that place.

—ALICIA KEANE

IT'S COMMON TO FEEL LONELY, to think of yourself as something small and solitary in the vastness of things. It's easy then
to think of a friend as a home territory carved out of that vastness, a kind of living diary for sharing and storing the feelings of
the day so that life can go on more or less as usual. Yet there are
other kinds of friendship that don't just assuage loneliness but undermine it by changing your understanding of who you are.
Friendships like this may be full of warm feeling. The friends may
be kindred souls, recognizing that human achievements are rarely

solitary even when they seem to be. But such good reasons are not the basis of this second sort of friendship, nor the source of its nourishment. This kind of friendship doesn't depend on reasons; reasons, after all, come and go. What is beyond reasons might seem to be incomprehensible, but there are all sorts of things that we do just for their own sake, because we love them, and some friendships are beyond any why. If you have such a friendship it can help you to find your own strength.

THE KOAN

On Mount Deshan in China long ago there was a community where two men had gone to take refuge from the storms of life in the outside world, storms of which they had firsthand knowledge. Though at first they appeared to be opposites, they became friends. As it turned out, one, whose name was Xuefeng, lived a long time and became renowned, but for many years, no one expected much of him. Xuefeng was talented at one thing; he was a chef and brought to the spiritual path a trust in hard work, precision, and pleasure. Otherwise, he was stocky, solid of body, and somewhat opaque in personality, as if a great, slowly heating energy in him kept the world somewhat at bay, while showing much about his motives and way of living.

Xuefeng hoped for an inner transformation though it was in no hurry to arrive. He persevered at what did not seem to be working—which in his case was meditation—since the alternative was ... well he didn't imagine the alternative. He was like the boy who doesn't have the knack with girls but doggedly persists in inviting them out. Albert Ellis, the psychologist, tells the story that, as a young man, he decided to invite one hundred girls out, since the refusals that met his first few attempts were obviously the result of unpracticed technique and a small sample. Both of these problems, he told himself, could be fixed by increasing the sample size. He went to the zoo, where he had noticed women on benches reading books. He too took a book and sat on a bench. He invited one hundred girls on a date. Not one said yes. So he decided that one hundred was itself too small a sample and embarked on another hundred attempts. The man in our story had longed for enlightenment for twenty-five years. He also decided that he had not given the method enough of a chance.

And this points to the deeper side of Xuefeng, which was that he had a feeling for duration, an appreciation that good things take time to occur. He liked to gather evidence to make the right decision, savored the slowness of gardens unfolding, of flowers and galaxies unfurling, of a mushroom sauce simmering and blending. He liked writing and remembered that the first written characters had come from the patterns made by heat when using a tortoise shell as an oracle. He wasn't sure that he actually believed that story, but, as a chef, it gave him a nice sense of history. For him, achievements came through accumulation, layering one act on top of another.

The other man in this story is Yantou, who was younger, and a kind of clown who claimed to be more enlightened than the teacher. He made jokes about religion, sex, and the toilet—which was not remarkable, but he and Xuefeng did live in a monastery. Some teachers secretly hope that such students will turn out badly, so they can say, "How impossible he was!" Yantou's teacher was old and indifferent to others' opinions and promoted Yantou. His clowning had dark underpinnings and seemed to help maintain temple life, which could be overly devoted to light. In 845, when Buddhists were being hunted and killed by an emperor who didn't fancy them, the teacher had spent the year in a cave, doing nothing much, waiting it out. Yantou became a ferryman and took people across the river. Gaining the other shore is a metaphor for enlightenment, so this was another of his jokes. He didn't take a crisis more seriously than, say, the weather. People admired this quality while privately wondering if it merely showed heartlessness.

Xuefeng genuinely liked Yantou. He was sure that Yantou was a kind of genius, far ahead of him in ability; yet he always felt completely accepted by the younger man. The chef believed that, just as enlightenment took its time coming, friendships needed time to deepen. He held Yantou in his heart as his friend and, when they were together, believed all things were possible.

Now, if you were Yantou's friend, he didn't share your emotions and the disappointments of love and work. You couldn't talk through a crisis with him in order to continue your life on more or less the previous, precrisis trajectory. Yantou wasn't useful for that. He didn't care about restoring normalcy. What he did help with was a change of heart. He was always willing to experiment on your mind. His empathy was not for your problem, but for the way your problem might open a gate. Whatever the differences in their approach, where you saw Yantou, you would soon see Xuefeng. Between retreat periods they took holidays together, wandering in the mountains, so it seemed clear that the friendship was mutual.

One afternoon, late in the year, they were being tourists, walking through a valley in Hunan. Yantou had a childlike readiness to be interested in everything—a chestnut tree, a butterfly, another traveler. Sometimes he had zero attention span, but then when he did fix on something, he ignored everything else. His lively face was relatively unlined. Xuefeng was as happy as could be with his friend. He looked straight ahead and stumped along, sweating, responsible, like a bear in a fairy tale, loaded with cooking pots. He liked to walk; he liked the load on his back and the feeling of weight that it gave to his life. Walking wasn't necessarily a means to get anywhere. To be in time, to wander, made time seem less of a burden, the present more enduring.

As the afternoon wore on, they climbed higher, more mountains appeared, and they crossed out of autumn into winter. There was gravel under their feet now. Clouds spread from the north, the wind pierced their clothes, and Xuefeng began carefully not to think about getting warm. Yantou complained and laughed and waved his arms about, and seemed to enjoy the change. By evening they had made it to the pass and Tortoise Mountain Travelers' Inn, which was really more of a hut. Its existence was due to carto-graphic whim; two provinces had boundaries there and a customs station was needed. Their room had a fire that vented underneath the brick bed that was the only furniture.

In the night, when Xuefeng went outside for a moment, it was very cold, and a wall of stillness met him. Large flakes of snow began to fall, as if he had awoken just to see them start. In the morning no one was on the roads, and he had a timeless, restful feeling looking out at the white expanse. The two companions ate rice and millet and regarded the walls. Yantou, having exhausted his jokes, rolled back onto his part of the bed, wrapped himself in the quilt, and slept. Xuefeng thought he could make use of this opportunity and sat up meditating. He settled quickly and didn't feel tired or bored. His mind was calm and spacious inside the little hut. He was concentrating so hard that he sweated and seemed to be losing weight.

It snowed for three days and three nights. Every now and then, Yantou opened his eyes, saw Xuefeng sitting in the firelight, got up, loaded the fire, and went back to sleep. Xuefeng thought that his friend didn't care much about duration, about the slow gathering of readiness, and didn't seem to take time to decide or to learn. Yantou seemed like an anthropologist, as if he came from a world in which time was not strict and life and death were not the main thing, just things, among other things. Yantou had once said that he liked to live, that just to live was enough, so—who knows?—perhaps even sleeping for days was thrilling for him. His kindness, Xuefeng decided, came from the way he relaxed and let time and the moment come over him. He didn't want to be other than where he was, and although he didn't seem to need much himself, he enjoyed bringing others into a similar understanding. Then Xuefeng drifted off into places where his thoughts were lighter than snowflakes and melted before he could grasp them.

On the third day, Yantou sat up and said bluntly, amiably, "Get some sleep! What do you think you are—a roadside shrine?"

Only the slightest threads of melancholy lay on Xuefeng, but they burned like the long streamers of a jellyfish. He touched his chest and said simply, "My heart isn't at peace. I can't fool myself. And I thought, up here, where it's so quiet..."

Yantou said, "I always thought you'd be a teacher, being so sincere and all."

Xuefeng usually took his friend literally since the other possibilities were too various to work out. The meditation was making

Xuefeng notice the visual oddity of ordinary things, their tendency to tilt into the nonordinary. His friend's eyes looked beautiful, not quite human, in the dim light.

"Well, since you ask, yes, I do worry, I get anxious, my life is going past me like a galloping horse. I get depressed, I don't feel that I'm of any use. But at other times, I feel clear, as if . . . well, there's not the slightest veil over my eyes, and then I forget again."

"Why don't you tell me? I can let you know if you're on the right track, and where you're not," Yantou grinned, "I'll whack your ideas away, prune the views."

Xuefeng took the invitation as a cue to describe moments of treasured insight, years of them, everything he understood about the universe. "Yes," he thought, "This is exactly what I need—to tell my friend and he'll understand." Once he began to talk, he warmed to the task and his yearning grew; his chest actually hurt. Each experience he described, Yantou batted away. Xuefeng couldn't protest. The stories were nice, but they were in the past. He was saying, "It was as if the bottom dropped out of a bucket," but the contrarian voice in his head was not impressed: "Where is that bottomless bucket now?" it asked. "The bucket still has fears in it." Yantou wasn't impressed either. Xuefeng saw that what had been significant at one time, a glimpse of a great happiness, was indeed real, yet it no longer had the power to soothe.

Xuefeng felt pale and wan; his balloon had been punctured. But even this emotion he saw as just a small, transparent doubt, almost a prayer; a tear, a raindrop, a glass bead. Without his achievements to compare itself with, his sorrow drifted away. A simple quiet remained. Then, into the silence, Yantou did something surprising: he roared. His roar, or shout, or whatever it was, was deafening in the hut. That's when everything stopped for Xuefeng. He didn't think "noise" or "loud." He didn't hear. Nothing was on his mind. Xuefeng shivered and shook. The hook from an old song looped in his head, "Anywhere else is too far away." At this moment, his thoughts didn't feel as if they belonged to him.

Then Yantou said, "Don't you know that the family treasure doesn't come in by the gate? Let the teaching flow out from your own breast to cover the sky and the earth."

These ordinary words hit Xuefeng like a blow in the chest. His heart felt larger than all of space; he wept and shouted. He yelled out for joy, "Today Tortoise Mountain has finally awakened! Tortoise Mountain has achieved the way!"

Yantou laughed, and thumped him and grabbed him, and they danced together. They danced slowly, with encumbered grace, while the snow fell quietly and the world was otherwise still. Then Yantou ate an extra helping of the rice and went back to sleep. Xuefeng didn't sleep but watched in happiness the whole night through.

Working with the Koan

What if it's true that real insight and joy don't come from the direction you expect such things to come from? If what you really want could come from any direction, that information might change the way you conduct your life. Instead of watching out for danger, you might be vigilant for happiness. Some people don't remember their dreams, yet if they try to remember, their dreams come gradually into awareness—at first a wisp, then a scene, and so on. They are learning how to walk in the dream's domain, and things that once seemed too small to notice become obvious. Happiness could be like this. If you were willing to relax with whatever came, there would be nothing wrong with sadness or any other difficulty. Since joy might be hiding anywhere, you would be willing to look with curiosity at sadness or fear, just in case.

Xuefeng's version of this strategy is to wait and let things come to him. When you feel sorrow, it might be taken as a request to sit down, right where you are on the brown Afghan carpet, and feel more of your own life. Or maybe you are happy, there on the brown Afghan carpet; it doesn't matter. Suddenly you hear, really hear, the Canada geese crying overhead. If you don't ask your sorrow to leave, or try to make happiness stay, either might be something merely present, like the snow on Tortoise Mountain. Then, both happiness and sorrow can be interesting and even, paradoxically, satisfying. Sorrow might be a sort of reverse Pandora's box from which, when you open it, happiness flies out. I might jump up and say, "Today the Canada geese have attained the way!"

There is a saying that everything we do is in the service of the self, and there isn't one—a self, that is. Xuefeng felt that he had joined his friend's world, because they now shared a language. Xuefeng saw the mountain as his own body and so it too became enlightened. That was rather a lot of a self to have but it wasn't personal or grand. What if he had awakened at the sight of a mouse? Would he have shouted, "Today the mouse has attained the way!"? Yes, he decided, he would have. What he had thought of as himself wasn't so important after all. He decided that this insight was what made Yantou seem so objective; Yantou didn't have an idea of Yantou that he had to groom and manicure.

Yantou's shout kept ringing in the brightness of the things around Xuefeng, who against all expectation became notable and funny. Thousands of people came to Xuefeng. Some of his students became great teachers of the age; some were transformed but lived invisible and anonymous, as Chinese dragons are supposed to—teaching calligraphy in malls. Others, of course, noticed no particular change in themselves. When people thanked him, he said, "It's got nothing to do with me." He seemed to regard teaching as an extended party with dark jokes.

Xuefeng did not think of his point of view as limited to his own body or his own personality, but he spoke also for the cities, the rivers, the trees. William Blake saw heaven in a wildflower.

Xuefeng said, "When I pick up the earth in my fingers, it's the size of a grain of rice. When I drop it, it might as well be in a black bucket, you can't find it anywhere. Hit the drum, call everyone to look for it."

Another time, perhaps when the piety of the monks was getting on his nerves, he said, "The whole world is a monk's eye. Where will you go to shit?"

When Yantou became a teacher, his character was as it always had been—unpredictable, indifferent to the things others prized. He was so clever that people just assumed that he knew what he was doing. When his temple was attacked, he sent his people away but himself sat in meditation in the great hall. Perhaps he was tired of the long war; perhaps he looked inside and couldn't find the thought of running away. A soldier rode in over the black and white tiled floor and killed him with a spear. Yantou had said that when he went, he would go with a great shout, and in the villages for miles around people claimed to have heard this yell; his last teaching, the same one he had given on Tortoise Mountain. When he was a friend he was a good friend, and when it was time to go, he wasn't the sort of person to hang around.

While the obvious theme of this koan about Tortoise Mountain is to point out the unpredictable sources of joy, the other theme is of the true friend. The true friend here is one who surprises or disturbs you in a particular way. As long as you are fixated in a particular direction, the friend may seem like a distraction, or even a nuisance, but when that happens he or she is probably doing a good job of being your friend.

10

The Great Way Is Not Difficult

Zhaozhou often quoted this saying by Sengcan:
"The great way is not difficult
if you just don't pick and choose."

LIFE *WITH* AND *WITHOUT*
YOUR CHERISHED BELIEFS

Everything is suffering for those who discriminate.

—Patanjali in the *Yoga Sutras*

I have four great vows:
When I'm hungry, I eat;
when it's cold, I put on more clothes;
when I'm tired, I stretch out and sleep;
when it gets warm, I like to find a cool breeze.

—Baiyun Shouduan

A KOAN SHOWS YOU TWO conditions for your mind: a *with* and a *without* condition. This is a natural way to understand things—life as a botox advertisement in which you are shown a haggard, careworn face, *with* wrinkles, and then the improved version, smooth as a baby's backside, *without* wrinkles. A koan uses this natural eagerness to compare things in an interesting way: when you work with the koan, what you are either *with* or *without* is your map, your cherished beliefs, your story about how your life should be at the moment in which you find yourself.

The *with* condition is what, in an unexamined way, you believe to be true. Beliefs have consequences; they build their own fictional world. When you believe something, you usually want the world to agree with you, to back up your story. Of course it rarely does, so your story will come with conflict built into its plotline. In the *without* condition, you see the world without wanting it to be different from the way it is. The *without* condition is an act of imagination. You ask yourself, "What might the world look like if I loved it as it is, just as it is?" Here is a koan that shows the power of imagining life when you are not depending on the stories you usually tell yourself. It also can show you what life is like in the *with* condition when your maps of the world vary from the actual territory of the world.

THE KOAN

Zhaozhou often quoted this saying by Sengcan:
  "The great way is not difficult
  if you just don't pick and choose."

WORKING WITH THE KOAN

Everyone knows that some events are just bad and make you sad or angry, and some are good and make you glad. Yet what everyone knows might not be true. For example there might be a certain coercion to the attitude that weddings must be happy, funerals have to be sad. It could prevent you from meeting the moment you are in. What if events don't have to be anything other than what they are?

Children laugh at funerals, some tears shed by brides are from disappointment rather than joy. Being fired or losing someone dearly beloved could open an unexpectedly beautiful new life. You might be armored against an unpleasant event that turns out not to be. Instead of wrestling toward what you are convinced ought to be going on, it might be refreshing to approach events without armor, meeting their nakedness with your own nakedness. That might also be a kind approach, since it sets up no conflict in your own heart.

There is a legend in which the Buddha comes upon the mind of not picking and choosing. On the edge of his own profound change of heart, the Buddha meditates all night under a fig tree, and an image comes to mind. He remembers that, as a child, while his father plowed a field in an annual ceremony, he was left in the shade of a rose apple tree. At this moment the boy has no minders around to distract him; he is under no one's gaze. His father is absorbed in plowing. The air is pleasant, the leaflight green, the shade cool. With nothing on his mind, the child does not want or fear anything. The sun seems to stand still. It is delicious to be alive. He feels a happiness not born of desire. The boy moves his eyes over the whole field. He can find no resistance, no tension, no inner conflict; everything is sufficient. There is nothing to add, nothing to subtract. And it occurred to him that exploring this approach, which he discovered in childhood, might be the direction in which enlightenment lies.

Here, not picking and choosing is something a boy wanders into; it is the natural state of an undisturbed mind. Then the boy notices that thoughts and feelings are always rising and that they are not themselves disturbing: thoughts and feelings are things in the world as much as flowers and parasols, and he doesn't have to either agree with them or quarrel with them. It's easy not to pick and choose about his own reactions, about his picking and choosing.

Everyone knows that Buddhism is about nonattachment, and people might think that not picking and choosing is about having no preferences. Yet nonattachment might lead to warfare with the part of you that enjoys the world. In this case nonattachment would be just another tyrannical belief and itself a source of unhappiness. Not picking and choosing could be the opposite of nonattachment, something more unsettling and demanding. If someone asks you, "Vanilla or chocolate?" and you notice that today you would like vanilla, and say so, that might be not picking and choosing. If you say, "I don't mind, what are you having?" then that could well be picking and choosing. You might be trying to guess what your host wants. You might want vanilla but be unwilling to reveal yourself by saying so.

I discovered something about this koan when my sister called and told me my mother was dying. I got off the plane in August in Launceston, Tasmania, to gusts of wind and cold rain. Water lay in sheets on the paddocks; the luggage on the carts was glistening. The hills were as green as in dreams, merino sheep had green seeds sprouting in their wool. My sister took me straight from the airport to my mother's bedside in the hospice. My mother, the doctor thought, was waiting for my arrival and might not last the night. "Dying of what?" I asked him. "Nothing, everything." He was a doctor who considered life and imagined that you might join him in considering it, too. He reflected for a moment. "There isn't a reason. She's just worn out." My mother was extremely wasted; her hair was baby fine, bone white, and drifted above her skull. Her skin had an uncanny translucence relieved by large dark blotches where nurses had tried to find a vein and she had bled under the surface.

I held her hand and sat with her. The next morning she was still alive, so I did the same thing. My sister was negotiating with the nurses about the oxygen levels. This was an intense activity. My father was trying to encourage Mum to stay in this world, to eat—for him, for life. "May I tempt you with just a spoonful of this custard, Alison? You might get a taste for it."

She was heedless, impatient, rude: "You don't know what you are talking about, oh you don't care, you have never listened to me, never!"

"Oh, Alison," he said disconsolately.

Everyone had something to do but me. I began to consider love. Immediately I noticed that whenever I wanted anyone to be different, the room filled with sorrow and pain. Under that condition, I began to struggle and feel terrible grief. There was nothing wrong with this really. It was intense and interesting, but my mother didn't seem to need it of me. My father or sister didn't need it either. It also wasn't something I needed. Then for whom did I struggle and feel grief?

I noticed that it was easy to think that my father should accept that my mother was dying and let her go. Acceptance, the last stage, and all that. And it was easy to think that my mother should bless Dad on her way out—why not? Or I could think that I should be able to help, sand off the edges of the conversation, oil the wheels. With any of these thoughts the room became small and fearful. There was a sense of strain, of needing to change others, of the hopelessness of that task, of picking and choosing. Wanting to change myself also led to this strain. This was the *with* condition—

with wrinkles, *with* delusions of control. But when I wanted no one to be different, the room was large and at peace. It was obvious in the "Why didn't I think of this before?" way that important things can be. Obvious seemed good. I didn't think my mother should live longer or that it might be better if she died more quickly or more painlessly. What she was doing was good enough. I wanted my mother to have the death that was hers and saw that only she could know what that was. And how my father kept her company was up to him. I could trust him to know what he must do.

In the *without* condition, it seemed likely that my father spoke out of love, and that my mother pushed him away out of love. In a long marriage, the codes spoken by the couple might make no sense to outsiders, including their own children. My mother's apparent attack on my father could have meant: "I've always felt oppressed and this is my final verdict on marriage." Yet she could just as easily have meant, "I'm so sorry to be leaving you. I'm doing my best, but I think I can't stay. I don't want to give you false hope." And my father's cajoling might also have been saying, "I'll keep you company as long as I can, so that you don't need to be lonely."

In that room, I did whatever came to me without thinking much about it. Mainly, I read aloud the slightly bleak, old-fashioned poets she liked—Matthew Arnold, Thomas Hardy, some Robert Frost. I read from an old grade-10 reader, *A Galaxy of Poems Old and New*. My name was written inside it in a child's script, and also the name of the boy who had owned it before me. Sometimes, as I read, I held her hand. It was the fag end of winter. Gales set in, and winds off the great Southern Ocean beat against the windows, offering a kind of companionship mixed with awe that seafaring people become familiar with. I was comforted by the wind roaring in the dark and confident that, as I walked, a path would appear. Everyone seemed to be free then, and the hospice room was large and kind, a peaceful place to spend a late winter afternoon, watching gaps of light appear, robins hop with twigs in their beaks, and then the rain bash against the windows again, the season beginning to turn.

Something else about the hospice. The story in our family was that Mum was often difficult. I had evidence, memories; psychotherapists had agreed with these memories. But after sitting in that room, not wanting anyone to be different, I didn't want anything about my life to have been different either. My sister and I started to tell each other Mum's Famous Outrages—the "Can you believe she did that?"—stories, but our hearts weren't in it. I noticed that, while I remembered the stories, my body didn't. I could no longer be sure what was intended in my mother's actions or my father's, or my own. It was easy to think that what had once been received as harshness could have been a step along one of affection's twisting paths. In the end, my mother defeated the expectations of the hospice and everyone else's expectations too. She came home and lived to see another Christmas. It turned out to have been an opera singer's farewell concert; a rehearsal for another farewell, at a future, unspecified time.

The night my mother died she was back in the hospice and I called her from California. I had no particular urgency and no sense that this phone call was more at an edge than any other. I heard her say, "Hello?" very sweetly and then ask herself impatiently which end she should talk into. She sounded like the colonel in an English mystery—someone intolerant of innovations such as shirts with collars attached and telephones that didn't need to be wound up. She knew that I was on the other end, but she couldn't converse and manage the phone at the same time. This might just have been the effect of a stroke she had had many years before. Her intelligence was frustrated when her body did not understand what was being asked of it, had no grasp of basic Tasmanian. It seemed that she was speaking into the ear end of the phone and listening to the speaking end. That is a likely explanation for the gurgles and thumps I was hearing in California. Like many human problems, it was absurd; the problem prevented me from explaining the problem to her. "Oh hell," she said, "bloody thing! I never liked it." By the clatter, it was clear that she had either dropped the handset or hurled it away.

I called back several times, thinking that she might by chance pick the receiver up right way around. But since she hadn't hung up the phone, the line was engaged. The nurse's station didn't answer. Before dawn the next morning I heard my father's voice come through the answering machine. "Mum died, John. That's all I have to say. Bye." I felt a love for him and also felt that my mother had indeed said farewell in a completely satisfactory way.

So those are my examples of the *with* and *without* conditions. With and without a belief about how it should be. There is nothing wrong with believing people should die a certain way and, for that matter, feeling the thrill of certainty that comes with any strong emotion, including grief. This too is life. If you don't dislike your own dislike, not picking and choosing is just present. It's not a discipline or a good thing that must be achieved. On the other hand, freedom is always interesting. When I was without what I should do and might do and could do, I just did what was obvious and was given to me. I experienced that as one of the shapes of love.

John Cage has a famous piece of music called $4'33''$ in which all of the notes are silent. While it has often been performed at the piano, the score calls for any number of people playing any number of instruments. Everything else that happens ends up being the piece. The cough, the siren coming up the avenue, your wondering if anything is going to happen, the air conditioner, your memory of church in childhood, your sense of waiting for something. What is really happening is always happening now. It's always now. What happens when you think something else is happening is what is happening.

My mother's funeral had another fine John Cage moment. My sister and I found that my parents' sound system was very old, and the funeral chapel system needed tapes or CDs, not vinyl. We searched through rarely opened drawers, finding cassettes of Highland flings and odd arias until we settled on a tape of a Vivaldi piece. I gave this to the funeral director, a pleasant man who had known my mother through other occasions. The idea was that, as we pushed the button to send Mum into the fire, he would start the tape and Vivaldi would fill the chapel. So we stumbled through our loving, difficult readings and tiny speeches; then the button was pushed, and as the coffin advanced solemnly into the furnace, dysfunctional squawks came like a shower of arrows out of the sound system. The tape kept trying to play and its clicks and grindings were amplified very efficiently into the overhead speakers. The coffin was gone. We could hardly back up and try again. So that was her music. No picking and choosing. The director confessed that he had inserted the tape wrongly. I shook his hand and told him that the ceremony was perfect. Everyone has her own death, and realizing this seems to allow everyone to have her own life as well.

After my mother died, I dreamed that she was walking slowly and with some effort along a path in the country. It seemed that she could feel my gaze. Yet, as if she knew that this matter was for her alone, she did not turn to speak, or ask anything. She met what rose up before her as a task, and now it was her task to go on foot into death. I watched her walk along that trail until she passed out of my sight. She seemed to know what she was doing. There wasn't any picking or choosing involved for either of us.

11

The Cypress Tree in the Garden

Someone asked Zhaozhou,
   "Why did Bodhidharma come from the west?"
   Zhaozhou replied, "The cypress tree in the garden."

THE TROUBLE WITH ANCESTORS

Learn about pines from the pine,
and about bamboo from the bamboo.

—MATSUO BASHO'S ADVICE TO POETS

S OMETIMES IT MIGHT BE USEFUL to step outside of the
stream of time and meet the minds of the wise who died long
ago. The Zen ancestors had stumbled on a method to change the
heart, and the problem they had was to pass on what they had
discovered. There wasn't an obvious way to do this, so they in-
vented koans. The idea is that when you spend time with the
koan, it will give back the radiance in the heart of the one who
made it. Koans might be imagined as vials of ancient light. There
is one strange thing about meeting ancestors in this way: when
they reach down across night and the years to give you their light,
you might find that what you have been given is your own light,
something that belongs to you. Here is a koan about what is
handed down.

The Koan

This koan begins with a man who wanted to touch something real and went to a teacher for assistance. He did not imagine that much of value might be found in his own life, and he thought that he had to reach far away and long ago to arrive at a starting point for the connection he sought. So he asked a question about a long-dead spiritual ancestor.

> Someone asked Zhaozhou,
> "Why did Bodhidharma come from the west?"
> Zhaozhou replied, "The cypress tree in the garden."

Working with the Koan

The setup here is that the man wants to connect to a spiritual great-grandparent. And Zhaozhou offers a tree in the garden, as if to say, "You don't have to reach so far away." Since the story of this koan begins with Zhaozhou, the teacher who sent the koan off on its long journey down to us, here is a little about him.

When Zhaozhou was a teenager, in the 700s, he left his city, a place called Lucky Image. Apparently, the real estate developer's impulse that gave California so many Paradise Drives is an old one. The boy made the trek to a teacher, called Nanquan, who was said to know something about how the world is put together. The teacher was lying down resting but, like a celebrity, receiving visitors and doing business from his bed. This sight was not something the boy had expected, and he found it gratifying; he wanted to feel that he was entering a new realm.

"Where are you from, young man?" the teacher asked.

"Lucky Image."

"So, did you see the image?" asked the teacher. Zhaozhou felt the conversation was already starting to tilt—which was what he had hoped for.

"No, but I see a Buddha lying down."

The teacher laughed and sat up, "Well, do you have a teacher, then?"

"I'm glad to see that you are feeling a bit better, sir," said Zhaozhou, and that's how he found himself a teacher. He stayed for forty years.

In his late fifties Zhaozhou went for a twenty-year wander, visiting other teachers. He liked standup routines, and one of his favorite conversations went like this:

"You're getting old—haven't you thought of settling down?"

"Where should I settle down?" Zhaozhou would reply.

"Well, I have a cottage I could give you."

"Use it yourself," and he strode off toward the next temple, the next conversation.

One day this familiar and enjoyable game took a different course:

"Aren't you a bit long in the tooth to be wandering about like this?"

"Where would I settle down?"

"Are you so old that you don't know?"

Zhaozhou laughed and said, "I've been training horses for thirty years, and today I was kicked by a donkey." According to the records, when he finally stopped wandering, Zhaozhou taught for nearly forty years.

You couldn't predict what Zhaozhou would do. When he was very old, the leg broke on his elaborate teaching chair. He wouldn't let anyone mend it properly but had a branch tied to the broken leg so he could continue to use it. He said that this was because he didn't want his students to waste time from their meditation, but no one believed him. A more likely reason was that he liked the broken leg, the splinters sticking out, and the rough branch bound to it. It made the chair more interesting. "This, this," he thought when he looked at it. He seemed to enjoy whatever was happening, and was a good host to whatever guest arrived. If it was cold, he enjoyed winter and the fire; if it was hot, he liked walking at evening. If he was happy, he laughed; if sad, he was just sad. He didn't clench up against life. Having a perfect chair was all right, but having a tree branch tied to the leg of the chair was even more all right.

Like others who enjoy being amused, Zhaozhou was a counter-puncher; it was good to ask him questions. His stories were tiny antistories, defeating the stories you might expect to hear, and his words went on working after a conversation was over.

Back to the koan of the cypress tree. You can come at it through either the question or the answer. First, let's take the path through the question. The legendary founder of Zen in China was the red-headed, blue-eyed barbarian from India called Bodhidharma. So, why did Bodhidharma travel all the way to China to teach? Or, you might ask, what stories do you carry out of the past? Who are your ancestors and how do they open or close your life for you?

Ancestors are people who were involved in disasters and tri-umphs, and who provide you with possibilities about who you might be. Even if you know nothing of your family and were raised in an orphanage, that is itself a noble ancestry that you share with many heroes and heroines. The result of having ancestors is *you*, along with your legends about how the world came to be.

When someone asks Zhaozhou about ancestors, he gives a sideways response, offering a possibility that wasn't on the surface of the question. He might be saying, "You are asking about Bodhidharma as if he were safely in the past. Yet you could meet the cypress tree, and your life, with Bodhidharma's eyes. If you hold this cypress tree up against your question, you will meet the old barbarian. You could go on your version of the journey he made, and make the discoveries he made. In the same way, Zhaozhou might still walk the streets of a modern city. A teacher called Wumen said that when a koan opens to you, you actually meet the ancestors: "Your eyebrows will be tangled up with theirs, you'll see with the same eyes and hear with the same ears. Won't that be wonderful?"

If you just see your own kitchen without fear and longing, without veils, then it could be intensely alive. At a moment like that, Bodhidharma is looking at the kitchen. When you look at the counters, the verticality of the walls, the window, the tiles, the precision of the corners of the room, the cypress tree outside the window, the branches of the laurel entwined with it and the pickup with big wheels parked in the drive, you are already looking with Bodhidharma's eyes. The thusness of things steps forward out of a surrounding darkness. Whatever you see might seem to have been present from everlasting, and to have an exactness, an emphatic quality of being precisely what it is. This is not the usual way to think of an inheritance: it isn't the armchairs and titles to land that are handed down, but the eyes to see with.

An artist found this koan appealing and carried it around with him day and night. He remembered his personal barbarians, his auntie in Los Angeles who drove a T-Bird convertible, carried a baby bottle full of vodka in the front seat, and came home at dawn in a black dress to crash on the couch in her own living room. He remembered his father who had been an orphan, then a policeman, and always carried a .45 in his pocket, and whose idea of good food was eating three meals a day. While he had thought of these figures as belonging to a life he had escaped, under the influence of the koan they began to change, became mysterious bearers of questions and kindness. He painted them as Buddhist teachers, versions of Bodhidharma, and wrote their stories on his paintings. Then he looked at trees. His discoveries didn't feel personal; he didn't think them up; it was just that while he kept company with this koan, a larger point of view appeared. He and a tree were both an act of imagination on the part of the universe. In some way he could honestly say, "I am a tree."

He also said, "With this koan there was a period when I identified with everything. I would go for a walk downtown and become the Styrofoam cup, the tree, the dog, the homeless person. I had always identified with the foreground of life, but now I was identifying with the background. At first I knew that I was the tree but I didn't yet know that I was Zhaozhou. I went to art school in the days when we used to sketch all the time. One exercise was copying the old masters. So we'd copy Leonardo, or Raphael, or Corot in precise detail. I started seeing things the way they did. With this koan I am copying Zhaozhou, and through that he appears, he lives again. It's not in some removed way—through fame or remembering. He actually becomes me the way the cypress tree does."

This man doesn't change his ancestors or clean them up; he sees them as they are. And as they are, they are beautiful, as beautiful as Bodhidharma or the cypress tree.

The artist's story brings us to the aspect of ancestors in which they are well known to be dangerous, hanging around where they are not wanted, asking for people to be thrown into volcanoes. Some of the earliest Chinese writing is on oracle bones and tortoise shells that were used for divination. A typical question was, "How many prisoners should I sacrifice?"

There is a tendency to think that the goodness of ancestors is necessary; yet that can't be true, since everyone has criminal ancestors somewhere in the tree. If Hitler was your ancestor, you bear no guilt. If Buddha was your ancestor, you bear no credit. The more you get to know them in a genuine way, as the painter did, the more your relationship with your ancestors grows and changes and becomes interestingly complicated. Genghis Khan is a national hero in Mongolia, though not in China. I have navigated using charts drawn by Captain Cook, yet he is not a culture hero to Australian Aborigines.

Spiritual ancestors have their own shadowy nature. The Buddha walked out on his wife and kids to look for enlightenment, and there was a Zen master who killed a cat to make a teaching point. And then there are certain eccentrics—the master who got enlightened in a brothel, the master who grew so fed up with teaching the emperor that he went to live anonymously with the beggars under the bridges in Kyoto but was eventually traced because he had a passion for sweet melons. The shadows of ancestors are not merely eccentric. Buddhism has plenty of men who loathed women, and the body, and plenty of warmongers. Ancestors provide the range of what it is to be human—the kindness and terror, the shame and forgiveness that you have to come to terms with to be able to bless your life.

The very darkness of ancestors can be freeing. Problematic ancestors can help you to take what is dark in yourself as something life has given you, something to make sense of, a gate into wisdom, and not merely a curse. Perhaps this is why Bodhidharma in paintings is wild and woolly, with a hoop earring, a beard, and intense, bulging eyes. These features are as much a part of his image as Andy Warhol's wig was part of his. Bodhidharma is the Beast with whom Beauty on the quest for enlightenment has to live.

Here is a story about the way that dark ancestors can be of help. A man was working on the koan "No" for some years. He noticed how compulsive the mind can be, and for him, to bring his mind back to the koan, over and over again, many times a minute if necessary, was to gain an enlightenment at the simplest and most fundamental level—to survive the debris of the mind. It can be consoling to discover that you don't have to believe in your own thoughts. He considered the poet Robert Lowell to be one of his ancestors. He said, "It is because Lowell bore an affliction— manic depression—terrible to himself and to those near to him, and he kept bearing it and did great work. That example helped my courage in bearing my own lesser hardships, my grief, and the way my own mind might turn on me at any moment." Mad ancestors can be a help in your own mad moments.

There is one more point that Zhaozhou is offering, which is this. The cypress tree in the garden might be able to reset some ancient grievances to zero. This is necessary since, if everyone needed closure for crimes committed in their previous lifetimes, there would be no time for living. In the Odyssey, after Odysseus has killed the suitors and the suitors' relatives want satisfaction, and the whole revenge cycle is about to start up again, Athena, the goddess of wisdom, intervenes. She threatens everyone and they make peace. It is as if they forget to hate each other, so that they can go on with their lives.

Here is a story about one of my ancestors resetting the family myth.

"You don't know who your ancestors are, do you?" said my great-aunt Mary to my sister. Aunt Mary lived in the nineteenth-century worker's cottage her grandfather had built; it was dark paneled and cool, and none of the walls was square. There was always a coal fire burning in the grate and a kettle on the coals.

"No, I don't," replied my sister hopefully, fluffing up her expectation, sitting down to hear.

"And you never will," said Aunt Mary as she tore the front pages out of the family Bible and threw them on the coals. Our ancestors on that side came to Australia in chains, and, in Aunt Mary's day, this heritage was whispered about as "the convict stain." To say that the past need not bind you was a large thing for her. And she wasn't really ashamed: she edited the family story in front of a witness. This has some of the paradoxical effect of Zhaozhou's cypress tree—as if she were saying, "The ancestors tell you not to pay too much attention to the ancestors."

Acknowledging ancestral stories and then seeing through them is part of becoming fully human. Everyone has to work beside someone who was an enemy of their own tribe in ages past. Everyone has an ancestor who did something appalling. The stories you have about your ancestors are stories you have about your own burdens and possibilities and capacity for forgiveness. The cypress tree koan might shift your stories about who you are and the limit those stories put on your happiness. You might notice that you get no merit from your good deeds, since they are done for their own sake. Also you are not a victim since no matter how terrible your past and how close you might be to despair, the moment of the cypress tree is here for you now. Zhaozhou's cypress tree might take away not the memory of old wrong, but the importance you place on your memory.

For this reason, Wumen said, "If you meet the Buddha on the road, kill him." Wumen brings Buddha to life and then disposes of him, the way my Aunt Mary did with our ancestors. When you do this, the ancestor leaves gifts but doesn't get in the way of using them. Bodhidharma can be someone back there and long ago and that is fine. Yet it is also nice if Bodhidharma is someone here and now. It's not a small matter to have a connection with the old masters, available when you need it. And if you open the vial of the koan, it could be that the light you see is the ancient light that was in their hearts. And it could be that just a little bit of light, a shard of light, is enough to change your heart; a little bit could be the whole thing.

As well as coming at this koan through the question, you can come at it through the answer. This is really quick. Zhaozhou pointed to the cypress tree to point to you. What is the cypress tree in your life? And if you, yourself are the ancestor, what will you do now?

12

The Bodhisattva's Great Mercy

Yunyan asked Daowu: "How does the Bodhisattva of Great Mercy use all those hands and eyes?"

Daowu said, "It's like reaching behind you for a pillow in the night."

Yunyan said, "I understand."

"Really? What do you understand?"

"There are hands and eyes all over the body."

Daowu said, "That's nicely put, but it's not the whole picture."

Yunyan said, "How would you put it?"

Daowu said, "All through the body are hands and eyes."

A SECRET KINDNESS
WORKING IN THE DARK

Meanwhile,
the great sea of compassion
rolled in, rolled out, rolled in.
And the blue mountain
of itself remains,
and the blind shampooers
never tire of their work.

—JAMES TATE

For now we see through a glass,
darkly; but then face to face.

—ST. PAUL

PEOPLE OFTEN THINK of love as an intention. Love's variants—kindness, empathy, and compassion—are also considered as traits to be cultivated. From this, you might think of love
as something that needs to be taught or learned, or in some way

added to your personality, or your day. Perhaps something you need to be happy. An accoutrement. Yet, if this were the case, love might die out, and it doesn't. This koan offers the possibility that love is what is left when you throw everything else overboard. The work of love is always going on beneath all the other moments, beneath even understanding and consciousness, at the bottom of the bottom. The Bodhisattva of love and compassion is sometimes imagined as having a thousand hands, to touch you, and in the palm of each hand an eye, to witness your life.

THE KOAN

The Bodhisattva's Great Mercy

Yunyan asked Daowu: "How does the Bodhisattva of Great Mercy use all those hands and eyes?"

Daowu said, "It's like reaching behind you for a pillow in the night."

Yunyan said, "I understand."

"Really? What do you understand?"

"There are hands and eyes all over the body."

Daowu said, "That's nicely put, but it's not the whole picture."

Yunyan said, "How would you put it?"

Daowu said, "All through the body are hands and eyes."

WORKING WITH THE KOAN

When all the stories about how to live fall away, what is left might be the real. But what about the human experience of the real? What to call it? What accurately describes it? What if the word might be *love*? When there was simple seeing, that would be love.

Catching a ball, that would be love, and picking up a child also. This would make love more basic than other experiences, placing it underneath everything else, at work in the blind night and the black earth. It would touch you and everyone you know at every moment. If this were true, it might make sense of the great intimacy and contentment you can feel just breathing and walking under boughs, walking through a spring morning—through the whole body, as the koan puts it. Sometimes it is hard *not* to feel linked in a great net.

One way to go with this koan is to ask, How often does reaching behind you in the dark occur? When I am working on a piece of writing or a painting and it has lost its flow, sometimes I fall asleep over the problem. In my sleep, waking and dreaming seem to thread through each other, and I dream new words or colors. That is reaching in the dark for what I need.

Another way to enter the koan might be to notice the touch of hands over the course of your life, starting with literal hands and moving outward from there. When you are born, hands catch you. Hands that can see you, taking in the softness of your skin and the way it melds to other skin. After that you greet people by touching hands, by embracing them with your own hands. I think of my mother cranking shirts through the hand-wringer, cooking her steak and kidney pies, making chocolate pudding out of a packet, drilling my sister and me on French verbs and Latin cases, and writing lesson plans in the evening for her first-grade class the next day. A thousand hands and eyes.

I think also of crimson and blue parrots hurtling in wave-patterned flight through eucalyptus trees, calling like slightly off-key bells, at the same time as a wallaby thumps the side of the house with her tail as she hops by. And here is a short list of a few other things that share the moment: bark peels from a snow gum leaving a smooth, white trunk running with red sap; a dented, short-wheelbase Land Rover whines and groans up the gray dirt track; a batsman hits a run on the cricket match on the radio; two children run out of the house yelling to each other; a large lump of asteroid sails by, just missing being pulled into the earth's atmosphere . . . well, you see the complexity. The working of the universe goes on constantly like hands finding other hands. Gravity, electromagnetism, and quantum mechanical effects go on simultaneously, and I think of the split-photon experiment in which if you change the spin on one particle, you alter another one, which might be miles or light-years away. That all happens like the left hand on the piano, without thought.

Sometimes, out of the corner of your eye, you might catch a little piece of the universe at work secretly. For example, in game 5 of the 2002 World Series, the Giants' first baseman, J. T. Snow, rounded third, and as he came home, the bat boy, the three-and-a-half-year-old son of the Giants' manager, ran excitedly onto the field to grab the hitter's bat. Snow hardly broke stride; he scooped up the kid by the back of his collar and carried him home. It was elegant, and automatic, and made it seem a fine, warm thing that the boy had wandered onto the field, finer than if he hadn't. There were all sorts of considerations—another runner was bearing down on home plate, and a ball might have hit the boy. Yet none of this seemed to go through the runner's mind; he just incorporated the boy into the play.

That is also part of compassion's action in the night; you can't be sure that what is happening is a mistake. You might find an unsuspected kindness in odd corners of an event or in yourself. If you are busy thinking that you should be kind, you might miss the reality that kindness is already present, in you.

As well as the multitasking that the universe seems to be so fond of, there is the thusness of common things, the way that, when you look at objects without prejudice, they seem to carry a brightness inside. There is a Tibetan meditation in which you imagine yourself to be that Bodhisattva of Great Mercy with all those arms— and eleven heads to boot. And imagine, too, that everyone you meet is also this being. In the koan even an inanimate thing, a hill or a stream or a car, might be one of those hands and eyes.

Here is how a woman in northern California explained this feature of the koan. She called it kinship:

> When I realized that I was seeing the world as it is, that led to the feeling of kinship. Whatever I paid attention to, that seemed to be me at that moment. I'd already been everything, done everything, owned everything. I'd already been this wall and this couch. All you have to do is be you and everything comes to you. It is not a question of ownership. The idea of something shiny and bright that I need to have is silly.
>
> The reverse is that I get what I want, I'm at home in this world. What I do is enough. One day I was untangling a friend's daughter's hair. Untangling went on and on, it became touched with light, and my hands were moving straight through time. I could see the thusness of her hair.
>
> When my baby was born, I loved him exactly as he was. It was a movement in the dark, before the light of thought struck the world. When a friend's baby seemed

to be dying, at first she and I were very upset; but this was abandoning the baby just when the baby most needed company. And we could see that we had to love the baby just as it was, even if we were to lose it. Though in the end we didn't.

Another way this koan appears is when the world reaches out for you when you have not asked it to do so. There's an old story about being touched in this way, a story from China twelve hundred years ago. Lingyun was wandering in the mountains and became lost in his walking. He rounded a bend and saw peach blossoms on the other side of the valley. This sight awakened him and he wrote this poem:

> For thirty years I searched for a master swordsman.
> How many times did the leaves fall
> and the branches break into bud?
> But from the moment I saw the peach blossoms,
> I've had no doubts.

Centuries later the Japanese teacher Keizan tried to help out by writing his own poem:

> The village peach blossoms didn't know
> their own crimson
> but still they freed Lingyun
> from all his doubts.

There is always the chance that the world might reach out its hand, no matter how late the hour. Even if you have no strength yourself, working with the koan could mean resting in what is true. Then it is up to the koan to do the work, to show you what it was made to do and why it was sent down over the long years to lodge in your heart.

The world can reach out for you, without thought or plan and, in reaching, reach into your depths. If you have ever sat quietly listening to the sound of the rain, you might have had the experience that after a while you can't tell what is rain and what is you. It can be an intimate sound, as if the rain were falling through your chest. Sometimes in winter, when I am alone in the house and my child is asleep, I go out and stand looking at the stars. The great horned owl gives its four-note call, and the sound goes through my body in the same way that rain can. And the owl call is enough. There is no flaw in the world. At such times, no matter how solitary you might be, it seems impossible to be lonely, because you are there. And the owl, the black eucalyptus trees, the stars and the flashes of light from automobiles—it is as if they are inside your chest too.

Throughout the whole body of the universe, hands and eyes.

The way things can happen by themselves, without being made to happen, is a strange thing, when you begin to notice it. When I first worked with this koan, I remembered drifting in a canoe off the Trobriand Islands, east of Papua New Guinea, sick with fever. I was delirious and hallucinating, and noticed that my mind was in a thousand pieces, and my body too seemed to be in bits. I had been reduced to matter. Occasionally, women who were diving from other canoes appeared, gave me water, and disappeared. To me they were hands and voices and faces. I couldn't knit the bits of me back together—the world would have to do that for me. And it did, though it might not have. For me, there are levels of the thousand hands and eyes in this story. I was apparently in pieces and each of them a hand or eye, preserving itself independently until such time as the whole could thread itself back together. Then there were the hands of the women offering water, the mercy of the world, another level of the thousand hands and eyes. When a problem is intractable and you cannot conceive of a solution to it, you will just have to live through it without a neat story about how it is to be solved.

I remember in that canoe, when I came back to my normal mind, there was a slight reservation about what was normal and a slight nostalgia for the purity of a mind that couldn't fake anything or organize things into the almost true patterns that it had been accustomed to maintain. When the body is trying to survive, there is not the energy for the autobiographical fiction.

There was a kindness in that fever, and it still seizes me sometimes at night, unpredictably, stealing my opinion of myself as a respectable, daylight-dwelling person. The fever soaks my pillow, and then, half asleep, I reach behind me for another. The Bodhisattva's great mercy is to provide pillows for the dreamer as well as to reach for them.

13

The Woman at the Inn

There was a woman who kept the pilgrims' inn at Hara under Mount Fuji. Her name is unknown, and it is not known when she was born or died.

She went to hear a talk by Hakuin who said, "They say there's a pure land where everything is only mind, and that there's a Buddha of light in your own body. Once that Buddha of light appears, mountains, rivers, earth, grass, trees, and forests suddenly glow with a great light. To see this, you have to look inside your own heart. Then what should you be looking out for? When you are look- ing for something that is only mind, what kind of special features would it have? When you are looking for the Buddha of infinite light in your own body, how would you recognize it?"

When she heard this the woman said, "This isn't so hard." Back at home she meditated day and night, holding the question while she was awake and during her sleep. One day, as she was washing a pot, she had a sudden breakthrough. She threw the pot aside and rushed to see Hakuin.

She said, "I've met Buddha in my own body, and everything on earth is shining with a great light! It's wonderful!" She danced for joy.

"Is that so?" said Hakuin, "but what about a pit of shit, does it also shine with a great light?"

The woman ran up and slapped him. She said, "You still don't get it, you old fart!"

Hakuin roared with laughter.

ARE YOU AFRAID OF
THIS HAPPINESS?

Behind all this, some great happiness is hiding.

—Yehuda Amichai

Reader, my story ends with freedom; not,
in the usual way, with marriage.

—Harriet Jacobs

WHEN BUDDHA had his first intimations of his own enlightenment, a strange question arose in his mind: "Are you
afraid of this happiness?" Happiness requires a certain surrender.
You have to give up your idea of happiness in order to discover
what happiness is. It's like the child not thinking about riding
a bicycle when he's learning. Okay, that's not overwhelmingly
hard, now, is it? Wait, there's more. Your unhappiness is threaded
through your idea of *you*. Happiness would overturn some things
you know about yourself. Happiness asks, "Are you willing to be
a different you?" Or, "Are you willing to be *not you?*"

Another way to say this is that happiness might be right under your nose at this minute. If it is not here, then it is not anywhere. Happiness is a risk to the self you know, because it doesn't require your familiar plotline. When people need a change of view, sometimes you have to take them far away from their lives and their own plotlines in order to find a moment when they forget who they are. It is also true that when you go far away, you may find that the place is very like home, though with the addition of, say, camels or kimonos, and that we travel in order to be more intimate with our own lives. Here is a koan in which we as readers can go far away, to an inn on the Tokaido Road, between Tokyo and Kyoto in the late 1700s. It's about someone who managed to forget who she was while in her own kitchen, perhaps a longer journey than the one we take to meet her.

THE KOAN

A woman ran the inn at a station on the pilgrimage route at Hara, a village under Mount Fuji. No one remembers her name, but she had a great awakening in her own kitchen. Her eyes looked directly at you, and she made up her own mind about things. Both men and women felt at ease in her company. Her turn of thought was practical and she liked to cook, clean, sew, and do. Every year she salted plums. She made vinegar out of persimmons from her old trees. She cut up radishes and cucumbers and put them in pickle jars, adding vinegar, spices, and seaweed that she gathered. She enjoyed the smell of rice cooking and the vigor of steam. In autumn there were pears; in late autumn, chestnuts.

Light seeped through the paper windows, the old brown wood wrapped around her like the fabric of a well-worn kimono, and she was happy. This was the point of being human, she thought—to have her hands inside the world, moving its colors and shapes. Her children grew and her life unfolded, placid, then shocking, then placid again. A son died of tuberculosis, a daughter sang beautifully. When travelers tied on their sandals in the mornings, they departed into the stories they had come from, and sometimes she longed to step into a story herself. Her thoughts went out to Edo, as Tokyo was then called, and even to Holland, home of the foreigners who were allowed only onto an island in the harbor of Nagasaki to trade.

One year there was a cold spell and the life she had known began passing from her like autumn leaves. She didn't know why—perhaps her older children growing up and leaving home left a void, perhaps there was no reason. In any case, the plum blossoms stepped back behind an invisible barrier so that they didn't pierce her heart that year. Slights enraged her; she woke fuming in the small hours. When a guest asked for a small service she told her, "Get it yourself." Her husband worried about soldiers breaking down the doors, and about a killing at another station up the road, but she was inclined to laugh. Sometimes she felt so much that she could hardly breathe. Her husband thought it might be grief over the loss of their son. But it wasn't grief. If she had known a spell to undo her pains, she wouldn't have said it.

What she felt was not an accident. She had always known that sooner or later she would have to face such a moment. She knew about the poet Basho, a wanderer who walked the Tokaido Road fifty years before. When she opened one of his books, the first thing she read was a poignant account. Basho had come upon a two-year-old running along the highway in distress, crying and hungry. The child's family couldn't feed another mouth and had turned him loose until his life should vanish like the dew. Basho wrote, "I threw him some food from my sleeve as I passed," and he wrote this poem too—as a gravestone:

You've heard a monkey shriek—
for this abandoned child,
what is the autumn wind like?

The poem released something in the innkeeper. She hugged her breast and felt the cry in her own body. She thought that although she didn't want to go down the road her guests took, a journey was definitely called for. As she went about her work she listened for a voice, a direction.

The inn had one treasure, a piece of calligraphy with the character for long life, given to someone by the local Zen teacher, an eccentric named Hakuin. The writing was beautiful though amazingly rough, and she felt alive when she looked at it. "The person who understands that roughness," she thought, "might know what is happening to me." When she went to hear the old man the hall was packed, and he made her laugh. It turned out that he was famous, though not, apparently, pious. She began meditating a bit, sitting and breathing, or concentrating on washing the endless dishes that made up an innkeeper's life. This meditation didn't seem to be a new direction but perhaps it was a condition for a new direction. She found a little more space between her thoughts, the trees began to step near again, and she calmed down for a while. But she knew that it was a temporary lull and that her journey, not yet begun, waited inside her.

Hakuin's talks were a mixed bag. They confused her, she went to sleep, she grew sullen and argumentative. Her skin itched. Hakuin gave advice to great ladies and local lords, to samurai, fishermen, and rice planters. But it didn't sound like advice. He said things like, "Straightaway, the rhinoceros of doubt fell down dead, and I could hardly bear my joy." He had a lot of experiences like that. Sometimes he talked as roughly as a soldier and ranted about something that annoyed him—a rival teacher, say. He had a high-flying mode too, and one thing he said went straight to her heart. "They say there's a pure land where everything is only mind, and that there's a Buddha of light in your own body. Once that Buddha of light appears, mountains, rivers, earth, grass, trees, and forests suddenly glow with a great light. To see this, you have to look inside your own heart. Then what should you be looking out for? When you are looking for something that is only mind, what kind of special features would it have? When you are looking for the Buddha of infinite light in your own body, how would you recognize it?"

The Buddha of light wasn't interesting to Hakuin's funding sources, but he was someone the poor country people prayed to for a good rice harvest, for freedom from bandits, for children and grandchildren, and for lower taxes. For the innkeeper, the words were spoken just to her. She said to herself, "This isn't so hard." She had finally discovered a wish that had been secret even from herself. She wasn't confused any longer, and she didn't try to think through what Hakuin meant; she just wanted to spend time with the koan.

She told her family, "I feel that happiness is as near as my skin," and she brought Hakuin's words to mind when she was awake and even during sleep. "Inside your own heart. Trees shine with a great light." The words accompanied her everywhere. Her husband asked if she had become a fanatic, but she wasn't in the mood for jokes. "This isn't about you," she muttered, and he knew that she was right. After that, he tried not to get in the way and to help unobtrusively. He hoped that she would find what she was looking for.

Meanwhile, if the trees emanated a light she certainly couldn't see it. But gradually she began to feel a connection with the things around her—a wooden rice bucket quivered with life, the doorway made a perfect doorway. At birth she had been given a doll, made just for her and, as a child, she believed that her doll danced at night. She could never catch it dancing, but in the morning it was more alive. The rice bucket was like that; whenever she looked, it had just stopped dancing. This connection wasn't really a light, but wasn't not a light either.

One day as she was washing a pot, she had a breakthrough. Breaking through into what, into where? She had washed thousands of pots, but her life was in this one. She was just scrubbing, actually, when she completely forgot herself, forgot her chapped hands and her wet clothes and what kind of thoughts she was having. There are dreams so deep that on waking the dreamer can't at first remember her name or where she is. Or even what she is. It was like that for her: the walls, the bowls, and her own hands were utterly strange and new. The moment had no end, and she didn't know which of her worlds was the dream.

She saw daylight coming out of the bottom of the pot and reasoned carefully to herself that this couldn't be true. The sunlight wasn't just in the pot; when she looked around, everything was bright: the paper screens, the tatami mat floor, the sound of a harness jingling outside, the smell of daylight. That was the particular feature of her change of heart—she saw things glowing with light. It was as if they had a song of their own, and that song was light. She began to laugh and couldn't hold it back. Her youngest child came in to stare at her enthusiastically, wondering if she had gone mad. But the woman's laughter set her moving out of the kitchen at a run. She tossed the pot aside and rushed to see Hakuin. She couldn't wait to tell someone who understood. By the time she got to his place she had settled into a jog. Hakuin happened to be sitting on the steps outside his room, looking at nothing in particular. As soon as she saw him, she began waving her arms. As if words would bridge the gap that was still to be covered, she shouted, "Hey!" and started babbling.

"I've met Buddha in my own body—everything is shining with a great light! It's fabulous!" It occurred to her then, as she ran, that she could test each thing she saw against her happiness. She could test digging the ground on a cold morning and the happiness was there. She could test her sorrow over her lost child, and when she did, she felt the warmth of her love for him, and then his life seemed complete. Brightness fell about her. She tested an angry soldier. Fine. She tested a dark, bent cypress. Each thing she saw had become perfect, and without flaw. She looked at Hakuin's face, and saw the creases of age along with the amusement that often seemed close to the surface with him. The light was in him too. She danced with joy.

Hakuin had the general attitude, "If you've seen one enlightenment, you've seen them all," but he liked what was irrepressible, including this woman. He stopped looking at nothing in particular. She felt him open to her and meet her delight with his. He came straight at her, "Is that so? But what about a pit of shit—does it also shine with a great light?"

She jumped up and down like a child. A test! A test! It was the test she had just given herself. "Of course, of course," she thought, "even shit gives off light, there is nothing that doesn't. And he pretends that he doesn't see." She enjoyed Hakuin's mind so much that she went up to him and slapped him and said, "You still don't get it, you old fart." Her thoughts were not really thoughts; they just appeared without her intending them. They formed themselves a little like this: "I see you, I see you. So, does my slap give off light?"

Hakuin roared with laughter.

WORKING WITH THE KOAN

Your own kitchen might be a good place for a deep change of heart. There was a Chinese woman called Yu who had her big experience while she was making donuts. She hurled the pan onto the ground. "What are you doing?" cried her husband.

"This isn't your realm," she replied and ran off to see her teacher the way our innkeeper did.

Pots and knives are among the first things humans ever made. A koan is sometimes imagined as a knife, cutting through every thought the mind brings up, pruning the vines. When someone works hard to concentrate and cut off the branching paths of a given moment, that metaphor seems to fit the method. Bodhisattvas of both sexes often wield swords with as much glee as a knight of the round table at a joust.

It could be just as interesting to imagine a koan as a pot or a vessel. In this approach you would embrace whatever happened as something belonging to the koan. Whatever joy, memory, celebration, or desire happens—into the pot it goes, to get cooked and transformed.

A sculptor said:

> The koan's been working on me, and I on it. For a while,
> I've been working on the idea that the koan itself is a
> container, like this: "I don't need to work on anything
> else, just these words of the koan; I don't need to fall
> apart if I'm having a bad day." The big negative emotions
> aren't scaring me. I like to see how they feel in my body
> rather than thinking that I should fix them. And I've
> been sensing the body analogy to the koan as well.
> There's a place in my middle that gives a lot of internal
> support and energy. Strangely it also seems to be a place
> where I can anchor the koan. And I've been finding self-
> confidence. The voice that enjoys and appreciates the
> art that I make is getting much stronger. I'm finding
> many things easier.

If you are working with the pot metaphor, you don't have to inter-
fere with your thoughts or feelings. You needn't approve or disap-
prove of them. This is not the moment of pruning; it's more like
the moment of making wine. Compassion has to start somewhere,
and embracing your own life is itself the beginning of a change of
heart. Some people do speak of a koan as a lover in their arms.

If this koan of the innkeeper appeals to you, you might want
to notice whether you can see the light in the most ordinary of
places. Can you find the light in your own kitchen? Can you find
it in your own body? Where is the light in your own face? At what
point in your life are you certain that there is no light? Is it painful
to hold that belief? You might try to point out the light to a child.

Hakuin's question about the pile of shit is just a version of, "Can you bear to be this happy?" And, "Can you find this beauty in all circumstances? Or, is there instead some part of your life that you think of as a pit of shit, a place where you never expect to meet happiness?"

As people change they often mention, with apologies or amusement, that the toilet has suddenly become beautiful to them, shit is fine, piss is fine. I take it as a measure of the feeling that no part of life is without tenderness and intimacy.

You also might find it interesting to consider the name of the woman at the station inn. This is a good question to ask yourself, because it makes no sense, since the name of the woman is the one thing about her that we are not given. So you have to use all your resources and rely on what you don't know. Does the unknown name speak to you? If you can find the innkeeper's name, you might be able to get her to dance. If you can find Hakuin's laughter, you can be amused yourself.

The woman's discoveries were about her own nearness to things. If you have empathy with someone, you join them; for a moment, you have the same heart. If you have the same heart as someone, you know their name. If you assume that there really is a light in your own kitchen, then you probably notice that sometimes you can see it. Sometimes nothing is needed, and you are not afraid of any happiness.

When you can't see the light in your own kitchen, could it be because you are making things small, measuring your life in coffee spoons? Buddha's question to himself, "Are you afraid of this happiness?" implies that we can be afraid of happiness. Happiness is a great risk to your own sense of yourself. You have to forget who you are in order to be happy, or to do anything whole-heartedly. Often what you might think of as yourself is a list of problems and achievements, particularly problems. Without a problem, you wouldn't need anything. You could lose your citizenship in the society of people who need things. If you have a problem, you need closure, or revenge, or to understand your mother, or to have your partner meet your needs. Yet most of these things are extremely unlikely to occur. And not one of these things would bring happiness if it did occur.

On the other hand, if you forget what you know about yourself, you will still pay your mortgage and love your child. When the beliefs fall away, what is left really does look like love. Here's a modern account of the discovery of light in the kitchen.

Maybe the first thing that happened was that everything was looking back, everything was responding to me seeing it. And the understanding, the feeling that we were not separate—we are in the sweetest awesome relationship to each other, family. This was absolutely engaging, whether it was a friend's luminous face summoning me to the interview line, or the door, ajar, on the porch. One night I was on my way back up to the lodge. It was raining and dark and I had this tiny flashlight. When I flashed the light, whatever I saw engaged me, a leaf, a piece of bark, the rivulets in the road. It took me hours to get home and I was really wet. So I spent a lot of that night on the road. But it was the same by day in the kitchen or the meditation hall. There was very little awareness of time and I felt no pain. Not the usual morning arthritis pain, no pain from sitting, in the back, or shoulders.

One test was with my sister, who had always been critical of my perspective. Connecting with her was a dearest wish, but I had long since given up thinking how to pull it off. Then everything changed. One minute there was the horrible, cavernous relationship we've had all my life. Then poof! It was fine. She called me up out of the blue to tell me what color she is painting her new house. "That's a great color," I said. I was happy for her. The next day she called to tell me about something she was going through. I listened. The next day she called me up to tell me she loved me. She calls me every few days now.

The only thing I can imagine about the change with my sister is my perception. But it wasn't announced; it had to be felt. Love, there is so much love. You see it. You see that bird over there, and at the same time you feel it walking in your heart. It's not just the birds; everything is walking in your heart. I never had really put the words love and Zen together in the same sentence. Look in Zen literature, it's not there really. Then I learned, I heard the word *intimacy*, and that does show up in the literature. It's a perfect word because it carries the ideas of love and respect and awe. And the awe is huge.

Later, I asked her, "What was the strangest thing about love that you noticed?"

She said, "You know I'm not exactly what you would call the Zennie Poster Girl. I'm fat, color my hair, and never understood koans before. I'm not cool. So if our ancestors so graciously show up for the likes of me, I think we can say they'll be there for just about anybody."

"I'm Tasmanian," I said, "I know what you mean."

When you are not afraid to forget who you are, life in the kitchen, or life in the office, might contain huge and overwhelming happiness. Everything you look at, the door, the walls meeting in the corner of the room, the light shining on the cell phone, might be so alive that it looks back. Other people might not be who you thought they were. Family members might be as fresh and surprising as strangers. And you, whom you have only apparently known all your life, might be fresh and surprising to yourself too. You might not have a perspective for someone to criticize. You might no longer know what you could not do. You might be an owl or an oak tree for a moment, depending on what the world shows you. And finally, when you are not afraid of your happiness, you don't get in its way.

I have a friend, a woman who said, "Oh, for me it was as if I stepped into God's living room. Trees and cliffs. It was simple, I stopped knowing what I couldn't do or live up to."

"Then what did you decide to do?"

"Oh, to get married. Will you do the ceremony?"

14

There's Nothing I Dislike

Linji said,
    "There is nothing I dislike."

ON AVOIDING BAD ART

The first question I ask myself when something doesn't seem
to be beautiful is why do I think it's not beautiful? And very
shortly you discover that there is no reason.

—John Cage

A MOTH IS A MAPMAKING CREATURE. When it flies into a
candle it is working from an erroneous map. Perhaps the
moth's map says something like, "Mating opportunities here." A
human is also a mapmaking creature. Everyone operates from a
map, and the map is always getting out of date. Life, the territory
described by the map, moves quickly. This means that the map
drifts away from the territory, eventually becoming more of a free-
standing artifact than a useful guide. When there is a wide gap between the map and the world, the person who made the map feels
discomfort. It has been a nice map and worked well for fifty years
or five minutes. And now it doesn't work. Some data are discon-
firming the map. In this situation, unlike moths, humans have two
choices. One is the path of discovery, in which the map is abandoned or redrawn over and over again. The other path is the one in

which the more doubts you have about a map, the more strongly you insist that it is accurate. This is the moth's path. Because you are a human being, if you follow such a path, you will be in conflict in your heart. Sometimes it is helpful to think of maps as stories, fictions, artworks. Making up stories doesn't seem avoidable. Stories just appear in the mind, bidden or unbidden, like the sight of a tree when you round a bend. There is nothing wrong with making things up. You blame yourself, you blame other people, you guess at reasons—these are examples of made-up stuff. There is a plotline, and what you are making up is drama; it is art. Yet if you think that this art is real, then you begin to suffer. You are building a prison cell to live in. It is the job of a koan to take down the walls of such prisons, to undermine your fictions. Then, you might discover that you are not really suffering from other people or from circumstances. You are suffering from your maps, your stories, your fiction, your prison. You are suffering from bad art.

THE KOAN

Linji said,
  "There's nothing I dislike."

WORKING WITH THE KOAN

What Linji says might seem unbelievable at first. If it's more intriguing to assume that Linji is talking about something real than the opposite, then what might he be talking about? It's easy to dislike things, but what does that mean, to dislike? *Dislike* could mean that you are feeling a strain between how things really are and your story about how things are. Since maps are always fictions, and always smaller than the territory, such a divergence happens every day. When it does, you might let go of your fiction or revise it. Usually this is not what happens. And when you insist more strongly on the validity of your fiction, you go down the path of disliking things.

This path of disliking things is common. It's popular in religion and politics and leads to what the Buddha called building the house of pain.

When a course of action isn't working, it's common to do it again only with more vigor. For example, some religions discriminate gravely against women. And, if you take no notice of the women in a culture, the men suffer, also. Everyone will be walking around in a trance, pretending to believe that their custom makes sense. Poverty will increase, science will decrease, art will wither. And what is a likely solution? You could restrict women more, perhaps stop them from driving. You could hold heresy trials for anyone who disagrees. Also you might make war to restore your dignity. Well, you see which way that path goes. It's called history.

When you dislike something, there is an alternative course to making war on the world or to hurling yourself once more into the candle flame. In this alternative course you might explore the fiction that belongs with your dislike. Exploration doesn't commit you to a stance; it just means that you look around. If you do this, you might catch the mapmaker, the storyteller, the paperback writer at work.

Here is a story about catching the mapmaker at work.

A man who sometimes had difficulty managing his mind took up koan work. Then, while in a retreat, he dreamed that he was in a war, a real shoot-em-up. Tracers crossed the sky, helicopter gunships laid down heavy machine-gun fire, men with assault rifles dashed by and took cover and dashed on. He could feel the percussion in the ground as the shells hit. In this hellish situation, he was fighting and shooting and found himself willing to try anything to stay alive. Then, suddenly, in the dream, he was out of his body and could see that he was dreaming. Behind his forehead he had a mesh screen, a mind screen, and the whole war with its desperation, anguish, noise, and loss was a film projected onto that screen. He gazed at the screen in wonder and relief. Instead of being a victim, he had become an art critic.

Then, with a whoosh, he was drawn back into the fighting. That is what it can be like to see through the fictions of the mind, the suffering made up of thoughts that stick to other thoughts. He saw that he was not his thoughts, and, as soon as he saw through the delusion, he was swept into it again. You might awaken and forget many times. Yet if you notice, just once, that the pain is on the mind screen, you will always have the possibility of remembering and getting free.

Here's an example of how fictions can make you unhappy. A man said, "I was abandoned and then adopted. It's terrible that I didn't grow up with my natural parents. That is the source of my problems with other people, especially women." Bad art is at work here, bad art probably backed up by psychotherapy to boot. And, at the same time, the way to undermine the fiction is clear. Fortunately the man made this claim to a koan teacher, who asked, "Why is it terrible that you were abandoned? What if your natural parents couldn't have managed? You could have died. And what is wrong with being adopted? Now you know that you were wanted. Your parents went to some trouble to get you. You were chosen."

"There is nothing I dislike" can work the way the koan "No" does. Whenever you are in pain, you can look at what you are thinking and see whether you really dislike what is happening. If your suffering comes from taking up residence in a world of what should be, or ought to be, then you can look at whether there really is a problem with the present moment. He left me. Well, if he wanted to, he should have. She betrayed me. Well, that's out of my control. It's good that we are not together anymore. There is nothing there for me to do. Using the koan like this can be very freeing.

Now here is what happened to a man dealing with something most people would find painful. The setup is this. His wife starts making long, private phone calls. When questioned, she is evasive or bursts into tears. They have two young children. The details are cloudy, and her story keeps changing. He is an engineer and likes stability in his emotional life. She confesses to having an affair. He tells her not to take this course and then realizes that you can't tell such things to adults. He thinks about their very young children. He believes that the children will not be happy or successful without a steady marriage. Images come unbidden: he thinks of the other man, and imagines his wife in bed with the other man. She won't promise not to see that man, then she does promise, but he doesn't believe her.

Finally he begins to sit still and notice. He notices that he is spending all his time on her affair. He is spending more time with the man in his thoughts than his wife is in actuality. As he sees through his thoughts, he notices that the other man is not present unless he brings him in via his thoughts. That he is spending all his time trying to influence his wife to feel differently. He also notices that this is something impossible—to control how someone else feels. And he notices that it makes him unhappy. What exactly does he dislike about his wife? Or the man she is involved with? He doesn't know the man and yet has a strong dislike of him.

The prescribed way to behave around such events is fairly set. Usually there is an obligation to be hysterical, to weep and offer recriminations. Recruiting the children is also popular. There is nothing to blame if you do this, yet perhaps it isn't necessary.

Then it is Easter Saturday night and the man goes to bed mulling whether he needs to keep his unhappiness. "There is nothing I dislike." In the morning he gets up. He doesn't tell himself that his wife is having an affair and therefore he must be unhappy. He doesn't tell himself any story at all. "Today," he thinks, "I won't have a story about anything." He can tell that this is just the beginning of a movement toward happiness, yet it is a great relief. He notices the impulse to make another story, in which his wife forgets about the other man and their children grow up in a united family and he feels like a good father. That is painful too, since it might not happen. Even a good story feels off the mark.

What is true is that he doesn't know what she will do. Also the matter is not only about her. He realizes that he is implicated too. He doesn't know what he will do either. He is not pretending anything, he is just not cultivating his pain and not claiming omniscience about what disasters will happen. Without a story he feels happy. Yesterday he was a man in misery, an abandoned husband. Today he is a man hiding Easter eggs for his children. His wife joins him. They are a man and a woman hiding Easter eggs for their children. They sit on a bench and watch. He can see that the children like finding Easter eggs.

The children don't have opinions about affairs, and they don't think about what should be happening. They do want their father not to abandon them for the sake of his fiction that his wife should be someone other than who she is. His opinions about his wife are not important to the kids. Then he notices that nothing is missing from the moment. He is a man sitting on a bench in a garden. Nothing is wrong. There is no flaw.

"From then on," he thinks, "who knows?" Maybe she will end the affair and stay. Maybe he, the husband, will leave her. Maybe she was right and he is the problem. Maybe nothing will change and the uncertainty will continue. What has changed is that he doesn't torment himself with his thoughts. He has breakfast, goes to work, comes home, has dinner, plays with the children, reads a novel. He lives. He does not require the moment to be different in order to be happy. He is happy.

Perhaps the koan "There is nothing I dislike," which at first might seem unattainable, isn't actually too much of a stretch. It might be just an observation of the natural state of the mind, the natural state of a man sitting on a bench, watching his children collecting Easter eggs, happy because he has given pleasure. In the *Dhammapada*, an ancient text, the Buddha observes how painful it is to live in the belief that you are a victim and observes, too, what it is like to live without such a belief. " 'He insulted me, he harmed me, he robbed me, he beat me'; if you think like this, you will suffer. 'He insulted me, he harmed me, he robbed me, he beat me'; if you do not think like this, you will not suffer."

The Buddha doesn't say that nothing happened, that someone didn't beat you, that no pain was caused. He is not encouraging you to pretend you are a robot, to go into denial, or to take up positive thinking. He just says that feeding the story of suffering makes you suffer. And he doesn't say that not feeding the story of suffering will make you happy. His words are a koan; they take away the story about suffering. How happiness appears is your business.

This koan raises the idea that freedom might be freedom from your own stories about life and who you are and who you should be. When you first see that you suffer from your thoughts, you might want to get rid of the difficult, painful thoughts and put good ones in their place. This is not the koan approach. What might it be like if you got rid of the painful thoughts and didn't put anything in their place? Then you might not be struggling to make the world fit your fiction. You wouldn't suffer from bad art. A man and a woman would hide Easter eggs in the garden on Easter Sunday morning, and their children might find them with shouts of joy. In later years the children might say. "I like Easter, I'll always remember that Easter when we were so happy."

When the Buddha made his discoveries, he said, "I have found the builder, and I will not build the house of pain again." Without your fictions, life has a simplicity that is full of beauty.

There is nothing I dislike.

15

The Master Song Man:
An Australian Koan

In Arnhem Land a singer named Maralung was asleep one night. As he was dreaming, a master song man from long ago came to him and said, "Wake up, I have a song to teach you." So Maralung woke up and the master taught him the song. Then Maralung went back to sleep and forgot the song. The next day a visitor said he would like to hear the song, so that night Maralung dreamed again and it happened the same way: The master came into his dream and woke him and taught him the song and again he fell asleep afterward. But this time in the morning he remembered the song.

Now, here is the question: Maralung knew the difference between dream and waking. So, was the master song man really there or not?

FINDING YOUR SONG

I have begun,
when I am weary and can't decide the answer to a
  bewildering question

to ask my dead friends for their opinion
and the answer is often immediate and clear.

—Marie Howe

If you ask whether you are awake or dreaming, the question itself makes life more interesting and resonant. A lot of things we do might be like finding a song to sing in a dream. If you want to solve a problem, your situation could be like the dreamer's in the koan. You don't have the song, and what's more, you are asleep. It all seems impossible. Then you notice something odd, and it makes you curious. There is an air of the uncanny and perhaps of danger, but you sense an opening and it makes you happy. This noticing is a kind of involuntary reaching out and when you reach out like this, without thought, your hand lights upon something. It turns out to be your song.

A song is a different way of communicating than, say, a memo. With our interesting problems—What about global warming? Should I get a divorce? How can I find a new job?—it's often not clear even where to begin. Problems start out looking to be either A or B and neither seems desirable. But if you see the problem from the back side or at another level, it may not be a problem anymore. That move is like finding a song. A song could also be the idea for a book, a solar energy panel, a way of helping a child in trouble—anything that you might want to bring into the world.

We don't expect the answers to our questions to come out of nothing. However that might be the only place a solution can come from. You start by not knowing—not knowing how or what or why or who—until that seems to be quite an acceptable place to spend time in. Then the strange thing is that if you reach out your hand, what you need might be there. This strangeness is at the same time encouraging and most disturbing.

Koans unravel the world that we have thought up, and it is this unraveling that makes it possible for a different world to appear. In the unraveled, unmade world it is not necessary to make yourself small in order to survive. It's fine if you forget the song that was given to you. You will remember it the next night, and if not the next night, then the next, and if not then, well, eventually. Error might not be a mistake, the song might even be improving while you forget it. The world's generosity is robust and persistent.

THE KOAN

The Master Song Man

In a place called Barunga in the Northern Territory of Australia, there was a singer named Maralung. He took dance troupes around to traditional places. The ghost of a master song man called Balanjirri and a bird called Bunggridj-Bunggridj gave Maralung his songs. The master song man lived so long ago that nothing of his life is known. In the outback you see mysterious moving lights, will-o'-the-wisps called Minmin; they are thought of as spirit lights and have their own creation stories and dreaming, but are considered to be dangerous.

One night Maralung was sleeping, watching a Minmin light. The light was blue and green and white and fell down across the sky from west to east. Balanjirri and the bird, Bunggridj-Bunggridj, appeared and set off after it. They followed the light and got a song there and then they came into the camp where Maralung was sleeping. Balanjirri said, "Get up, I have a song to teach you." The dreamer woke up and the master taught him the song. The bird sang too. The song was in the ghost language, so humans could sing it but only spirits could understand it. Maralung told the story:

> He got those ... what do you call them ... corroboree sticks. They just appeared there. They were enormous those corroboree sticks. Oh ho. Fuck me dead, they were huge. That didgeridoo player, he sat down about as far from me as that bloody chair. Balanjirri called the didgeridoo player "son." It wasn't a short didgeri-

doo. It was enormous. And he played that didgeridoo right there for me.

"Don't lose this song, you keep this one," said the old song man, "I sang this song for you. It's yours." He spoke kindly like that.

"All right."

"OK, you've got to remember it properly, this good song, this Minmin light of yours."

He went back and I continued to sing after he'd left. But fucking silly bugger, I fell asleep. But don't you worry, I'll get it. Maybe one or two, three, four, five . . . if he shows me . . . six, seven, eight, nine, that's it.

So the next night Maralung dreamed again and it happened the same way. Again the master and the bird came into his dream and woke him and sang for him and again he fell asleep afterward. But this time in the morning he remembered the song.

Now, here is the question. Maralung knew the difference between dream and waking. So, was the master song man really there or not?

Working with the Koan

When you need something, and you don't quite know what you need, you can get more than you have asked for and be drawn into a larger, stranger world. The Minmin lights are dangerous; the bird and the ghost go to a place where there might be demons, but that's where you have to go to get a song—to a place that is beyond what you have ever known before. That's why the song sticks that keep the dance rhythm are enormous, and the didgeri-doo is too. The things to do with the song are huge, the way everything is huge in Rabelais, the way there are giants in Grimm, and the way people are especially fierce in manga tales in which ghosts and demons mix with the living. The master song man and the bird together take risks to aid the living singer. That danger and weirdness might be good for our lives.

For a long time I felt cut off from the world, a billiard ball in a Cartesian space, and a gulf separated me from the fish, animals, trees, and people—my mind was not content or whole. There were symptoms, such as having more thoughts than I could possi-bly use at any given moment, and clumsiness with people, but probably the main symptom was of being shut out of the magic in things. I worried at the problem, studying animals and plants and noticing that all the steps I took did not help. Then one day the gap wasn't there anymore. After the gap disappeared, I could let a situation tell me what it was about, let people reveal themselves to me, without finding a problem. Sometimes wholeness is just given. It has to be given actually, because effort leads to effort, not to wholeness. So where does wholeness come from? Well that's one of the great questions. Where do we come from? Where does the universe come from? A ghost and a bird got it from the Min-min lights.

Maralung's story was told me by a musicologist from Sydney University, Allan Marett, when he came to a retreat in the bush at Gorrick's Run outside of Sydney. I taught there regularly for about twelve years during the eighties and nineties. Allan knew about Zen and Japanese music but had been studying the music in the Northern Territory, and he used to play didgeridoo at the end of retreats. He recorded some of Maralung's songs and they are on the Web. That song is called "Minmin light." Maralung spoke two Aboriginal languages; Allan talked with him in pidgin, which was his third language.

As I see it, the world arrives out of what is unknown and unimagined. Everything just appears as it is, coming toward us; it is a gift, not a product, and it stumbles over us, crashes into us, or comes to fetch us. I suppose it helps to show up without much going on in our minds. That's the discipline—the bit about not having much going on in our minds. It might be more accurate to say that it's not about whether there is something in the mind, but about whether we automatically believe our thoughts. However, having less going on in the mind helps us to be curious about our thoughts and to see the dreamlike nature of what we usually think is important. It's in the nature of imprisonment to believe that we are our thoughts. When we don't, freedom seems to have already arrived.

For Allan, the musicologist, what came to fetch him was the question "Since Maralung knew the difference between waking and dreaming, was the ancient song man really there or not?" I think we pretty much have to accept the form in which a question comes to us. Then we have to stay with the question. Any question that arises will open into others. A friend living in Lucca, in Tuscany, faced with the strangeness of the beliefs in miracles—the saint whose body never decayed and the enormous slab of marble dragged up from the sea by two oxen—asked the same question, Is this real? The koan "No" asks about human nature and whether it is the same as a dog's, whether we have a share in the mystery of life—a variant of the same question. Whenever I really take on a question of this kind, it looks like a wall at first, but it turns out to have more interesting possibilities than I first thought. There is often something humbling about realizing this, the shallowness of my initial reaction. The wall usually turns out to be a gate.

Most of the time there is a gap between the life we know is possible and the one we live. That gap appears as restlessness, pain, longing, fear, irredeemable loneliness, your skin crawling—some uncomfortable state. The koan's job is to take you across any gap between yourself and your life. It's not something to make sense of, any more than a poem or a piece of music would be. You can't set out to get a song, nevertheless a song might come to you.

Here's a story about how, like Balanjirri waking the sleeper, the world can come to fetch us, and take us across this gap. Nancy Farmer is a children's novelist. When she told me this story she was on her way to Germany to accept an award for one of her books. It turned out not to be a plaque or scroll but a shining metal sculpture, Brancusi-like and dramatically incomprehensible. She wasn't always a novelist, though; before the writing and the awards, she was a freelance scientist working for corporations. Then her employer at the time changed her job description so that it included travel. Since she had a young child, this didn't seem like a good idea. So she realized that she needed another job.

She had no idea what she would do, but had the sense that she was open to changing her life completely. There isn't really a clear path to changing your life completely, so she just more or less understood that it was a possibility and went on with her routine. One evening she was reading a book, a story for older children, when an image struck her forcibly. The image that inspired her was of a small boy (about her son's age at the time) about to walk across a frozen pond, fall through the ice, and drown. She realized that she knew where the story was going. "I could do this," she thought. She read on, and went to bed as usual. The next day she woke up and began writing her first novel. She said, "I became a writer overnight." The image did not seem to be important in itself, but it handed her across that gap into a new life.

The issue in Maralung's story is also about bringing curiosity to the whole range of experience, especially into situations that might seem alien or dangerous. Koans are meant to work in all conditions; we could assess this notion by testing it in a resolutely mundane environment that is also full of striving—the California bar exam. The bar exam is a barrier that attorneys have to pass in order to practice in the state. Like a lot of professional examinations it functions partly as quality control and partly, perhaps mainly, as a guild requirement intended to keep people out. The exam takes place over three days, law professors from great universities have been known to fail it, and it is universally dreaded. Rachel Howlett, an environmental attorney and Zen teacher, told me about taking the bar exam in Sacramento. The story, like Maralung's, shows the arc of practice, and how we might get home when we seem to be lost.

There were eight hundred people in the convention center, which has a concrete floor; the noise of the metal legs of the chairs scraping is one of its main design features. In this dreamlike environment, a dreamlike figure appeared. During the exam, proctors check the photos at the desks periodically to prevent you switching yourself for someone more knowledgeable. The proctor for Rachel's row was under five feet tall, an older, black woman with blond hair, who announced solemnly, "I bless everyone in my row. Every one of you is going to pass." One of her friends heard about this and asked the proctor to bless him too and she did, and he did pass the exam.

As the test went on, day after day, some of the effects of being in a retreat set in. A person's foot, a staple in a sheet of paper, or a section of a wall would strike Rachel in an unusually vivid and intimate way. Each object seemed perfect and absorbing. It vied for and held her attention. She would find herself in conversation with it, murmuring things like, "I'll look at you again later, just now I have to do this exam." The thusness of these things too was a call.

There was a multiple choice section of the exam composed of fictional plaintiff-versus-defendant cases in which the plaintiffs all have names beginning with P and the defendants have names beginning with D. Dirk and Daisy and Devonish-Meares are always mistreating Paula and Penelope and Pompey. There are 1.8 minutes to understand and answer the case and then forget it and begin the next one. Trekking along through these cases, she found herself in a timeless place. There was no future or past. She had always been answering questions about Periwinkle and David, it wasn't difficult to do, and in fact it was enjoyable as well as eternal. On the surface there was turmoil and striving and trouble, but underneath there was no problem at all. It turned out that she failed the bar on that first attempt, but passed on the second, like Maralung remembering the song. The proctor's blessing came true eventually. And a sincere blessing is something to be accepted; it's a real blessing no matter what the outcome.

The final piece of this bar exam story is also about how to move across a gap. On her second attempt at the bar, Rachel was dressed up and ready to go, waiting till the last possible minute to stand in line with the other anxious people, trying to manage her own anxiety, thinking, "I wonder if I can get out of doing this." We take our minds for granted, imagining that they will behave themselves, but they don't. It can't be assumed that we will think what we intend to think, and we don't always do what we tell ourselves to do. We might believe that we are our thoughts and feelings, but our thoughts and feelings are objects in the world, just like tables and mirrors. We might have to negotiate with them at any time.

In this case Rachel looked in the mirror in her hotel room and noticed that she was not really seeing her own face. She wasn't present to her image. She couldn't quite feel her feet on the carpet or the washbasin under her hands. "This," she decided, "is not good." She felt close to her life but not quite there, and not quite there didn't seem to be enough for the exam. "Is it possible to wake myself up?" she wondered. She tried to see what the extra piece of the situation was but she couldn't. She picked up the toothpaste, looked at her reflection again. She noticed that she was trying to stave off her nervousness and she must have stopped opposing herself, because suddenly she could see the gleam of the washbasin, and feel the carpet under her feet and the cold air on her face. She was ready. The way she crossed the gap was to be curious, to wait with the conditions as they were and not to find fault with them. She couldn't wake herself up but she began to pay attention in a deeper way and the waking up happened.

It might be possible to find our song, our course of action, ourselves, in any situation. This finding wouldn't depend on preset moves—it could be the wrong move that will save us. Here's an example of the way what is unlooked for and even impossible can change a situation. When someone dies we usually think that the verdict is fixed; that's it for their participation in life. But the master song man was still ferrying songs into the world long after no one knew who he was, so perhaps the verdict is not completely fixed after all.

When my mother's ashes came back from the crematorium, my family spent a couple of days staring at the plastic box that held them. Then we took the box to the old cast iron bridge across the Tamar River. Both bridge and river had been continual companions to her life. I undid a surprising number of layers and poured the ashes into the water below. But this wasn't the end; even after this she kept changing. I noticed the change because the quality of her advice improved. When she was alive her counsel seemed to be distorted by thoughts about what the neighbors might think, what her own parents had said, her view of her capacity to advise anyone, the fears of the day. After running through all these pipes and tubes, my mother's advice came out a bit perturbed, and as a consequence I don't remember consulting her very often.

After my mother died though, I noticed I could say something to her and a surprisingly clear, immediate, and satisfactory response would appear somewhere in my chest. She considered the most important thing—what might lead to happiness, how not to take things too seriously, how to care for others with a lighter touch. The virtues that she had always possessed were more visible. She wasn't interested necessarily in the course that would lead to fortune or fame. I got the impression that things were turning out OK, that, so far, so good. Her thoughts were not quite advice, but more of a surefooted sense of the flow of things.

Maralung went around from tiny place to tiny place, to little outback towns with a pub and a post office, to camps of bark lean-tos at river crossings. He would set up with his dance troupe and sing. Afterward, he would move on. Sometimes he painted houses for money. It seems to me a generous and consoling gesture to offer what you have without thought of how it will be received or what return the universe will give. That's what the ghost, Balanjirri, did, and the bird did too. There is a difference between singing under some eucalyptus trees at a river crossing in the Northern Territory, and being on the stage at the Sydney Opera House, but we can't say that the difference is always in favor of the Sydney Opera House. What makes a human life real and beautiful is available in every place. An insubstantial and alienated life—eating a hearty breakfast of a cardboard photo of corn flakes—is always on offer but its consolations are not consoling. In order to embrace a handmade life, you do have to be willing to deal with the Minmin lights along with awe and fear. But you have to deal with awe and fear anyway, and when you pay attention, a continual turning toward the genuine just happens.

We can't say that human lives have a purpose, since a purpose would be smaller than we are. It's true though, that the impulse to give freely to the world seems to be at the bottom of the well of human intentions where the purest and clearest water arises. To be able to offer back what the world has given you, but shaped a little by your touch—that makes a true life. Eventually we find our song and remember it and sing it. And we can never know who else will sing the song, or how the story will turn out in the end; its ripples widen beyond us and there is no end in sight.

Coda

Koans are still appearing in the world. Maralung's account tells how koans might come about—a long-dead master song man and a bird made a raid on the unknown. I have often imagined koans as vials of ancient light; in this image, when you get the vial open, the light shines out and everything you see shines too. You can also think about koans as conversations that come out of a dreaming, out of the place that art comes from, that the universe is born from, and that is a bigger analogy. It gives a context for new koans and koans from different cultures. Knowledge that seems dead might be refreshed. And that knowledge might help the world's endangered greenness to return also. You don't even have to go looking for a koan, since there's no way to find it. It will find you.

Notes

The koans are translated from the Chinese by Joan Sutherland and me, unless otherwise noted. Translations from the Japanese are mine, again unless otherwise noted.

Three koan collections, made between eight hundred and a thousand years ago, are still commonly used:

1. *The Blue Cliff Record* was the first of the great, strange, and poetic koan collections, and contains one hundred koans. It was compiled in the eleventh century by the Chan teacher Xuedou Chongxian, who added his own verses and remarks. In the twelfth century, Yuanwu Keqin, who lived and gave talks under the Blue Cliff in Hunan, added introductions and commentaries. A good translation is *The Blue Cliff Record*, translated by Thomas Cleary and J. C. Cleary (Boston: Shambhala, 1977).

2. *Book of Serenity* is another collection of one hundred koans assembled by Tiantong Hongzhi, who added his own verses. The later master Wansong Xingxiu added commentary and more verses. A good translation and introduction is Thomas Cleary, *Book of Serenity* (Boston: Shambhala, 1998).

3. *The Gateless Barrier* is a collection of forty-seven koans compiled by Wumen Huikai. There are many translations and commentaries. My favorite is Zenkei Shibayama, *Zen*

Comments on the Mumonkan, translated into English by Sumiko Kudo (New York: Harper & Row, 1974).

Andrew Ferguson also has a good translation of the records of the old masters: *Zen's Chinese Heritage: The Masters and Their Teachings* (Somerville, Mass.: Wisdom Publications, 2000).

(*Note:* If you deal with anything Chinese you have to put up with the fact that there are two common systems for writing Chinese in Roman letters, the most authoritative developed by Albanians during Mao's era and containing lots of words beginning with X. These systems offer two different ways of mispronouncing Chinese. Also the Japanese have their own way of mispronouncing Chinese.)

Introduction: AN IMPOSSIBLE QUESTION MEANS A JOURNEY

PAGE 3: ZHAOZHOU IN HELL A good version of Zhaozhou's koans is *The Recorded Sayings of Zen Master Joshu,* translated and introduced by James Green (Boston: Shambhala, 1998). Joshu is the Japanese way of saying Zhaozhou.

PAGE 7: QINGSHUI, ALONE AND DESTITUTE This koan appears in *The Gateless Barrier (Wumenguan),* case 10, as well as in James Green's translation.

PAGE 8: PAPER CLOTHING The master in question was Yunmen.

1. *Bodhidharma's Vast Emptiness:* FORGETTING WHO YOU ARE AND MAKING USE OF NOTHING

This koan is from *The Blue Cliff Record.* It also appears in the *Book of Serenity.*

PAGE 13: "TO STUDY THE BUDDHA'S WAY" These lines are from

Genjo Koan in Eihei Dogen, *Moon in a Dewdrop: Writings of Zen Master Dogen*, edited by Kazuaki Tanahashi (New York: North Point Press, 1995).

PAGE 13: "POETRY ARRIVED" Excerpt from Pablo Neruda, "Poetry," translated by Seraphina Goldfarb-Tarrant and John Tarrant, from *Memorial de Isla Negra*. A good translation is Alastair Reid, *Isla Negra: A Notebook* (New York: Noonday Press, 1982).

2. *Zhaozhou's Dog:* THE SECRET OF CHANGING YOUR HEART

This koan is from *The Book of Serenity*. It also appears in *The Gateless Barrier*.

PAGE 24: "TRY TO LOVE *THE QUESTIONS THEMSELVES*" Excerpt from Rainer Maria Rilke, *Letters to a Young Poet*, translated by Stephen Mitchell (New York: Random House, 1984), letter 4.

PAGE 24: GOING BROKE HAPPENS IN TWO WAYS Ernest Hemingway, *The Sun Also Rises* (New York: Scribner, 1926).

PAGE 25: THE LAMAS These were Lama Yeshe and Zopa Rinpoche.

PAGE 27: ROBERT CREELEY Joan Sutherland told me this story.

PAGE 29: MAUI This was Robert Aitken's training center.

PAGE 30: JAPANESE TEACHER This was Koun Yamada.

PAGE 32: A WOMAN IN NORTHERN CALIFORNIA This was Rachel Howlett. She later became an attorney and koan teacher.

3. *Rhinoceros:* MEETING THE INCONCEIVABLE

This koan appears in both *The Blue Cliff Record* and the *Book of Serenity*.

PAGE 38: The Red Queen makes her comment in *Through the Looking Glass*. Lewis Carroll, *The Annotated Alice: Alice's Adventures in Wonderland* and *Through the Looking Glass*, illustrated by John Tenniel, introduction and notes by Martin Gardner (New York: Random House, 1998).

PAGE 39: The stories about Yanguan appear in Ferguson, *Zen's Chinese Heritage*.

PAGE 45: THE METRO Mayumi Oda told me this story.

4. *Ordinary Mind Is the Way:* THE HEAVEN THAT'S ALREADY HERE

This koan is from *The Gateless Barrier*.

PAGE 50: BASHO'S ADVICE TO POETS This advice was his attempt to describe *karumi*, a kind of lightness that replaced *sabi* and *wabi*—the combination of loneliness and simplicity—as a guiding principle in Basho's teaching toward the end of his life. See Makoto Ueda, *Basho and His Interpreters: Selected Hokku with Commentary* (Stanford, Calif.: Stanford University Press, 1992).

PAGE 54: Philip Whalen was abbot of Hartford Street Zendo well after Issan Dorsey died. There were two Zen hospices in San Francisco. Philip lived at Hartford Street Zen Center, associated with Maitri, the AIDS hospice that Issan Dorsey and friends founded. Philip himself, not suffering from AIDS, was in the Zen Center Hospice on Page Street. Philip eventually died in the hospice unit of Laguna Honda Hospital. This unit had a connection with Zen Center Hospice.

5. A Condolence Call: PURSUING DEATH INTO LIFE
This koan is from *The Blue Cliff Record.*

PAGE 61: "MY BOAT HAS BUMPED . . . INTO SOMETHING BIG"
Excerpt from "Oceans," Juan Ramón Jiménez, translated by
Seraphina Goldfarb-Tarrant and John Tarrant. A good transla-
tion is in *Lorca and Jiménez: Selected Poems,* edited by
Robert Bly (Boston: Beacon Press, 1973).

6. The Red Thread: CONNECTIONS THAT DESIRE MAKES
This koan is part of the standard koan curriculum handed down
orally and in typescript. There is an interesting account of it in
John Stevens, *Lust for Enlightenment: Buddhism and Sex*
(Boston: Shambhala, 1990).

PAGE 74: "FRIDAY I TASTED LIFE" Emily Dickinson, quoted in
Ted Hughes, *Winter Pollen: Occasional Prose,* edited by
William Scammel (New York: Picador, 1995). I found this
quotation in *The Reader's Rejoinder,* a periodical collection of
quotations and reviews published through the 1990s by Don
Emblen of Clamshell Press, Santa Rosa.

PAGE 74: "WE MUST AGREE ON WHAT MATTERS" Salman
Rushdie, "Fighting the Forces of Invisibility," *Washington
Post,* October 2, 2001, A25.

PAGE 77: Issan Dorsey was the first abbot of Hartford Street Zen
Center. Ken Ireland, who for a time ran Maitri Hospice,
helped with memories about Issan. For one account of Issan,
see David Schneider, *Street Zen: The Life and Work of Issan
Dorsey* (Boston: Shambhala, 1993).

7. *Counting the Stars:* A BORING KOAN

This koan is part of the standard koan curriculum handed down orally and in typescript.

PAGE 84: "LOWER YOUR STANDARDS" William Stafford said this many times. Kim Stafford, *Early Morning: Remembering My Father, William Stafford* (St. Paul, Minn.: Graywolf Press, 2002).

PAGE 84: "NEVER THINK OF YOURSELF AS A PERSON WHO DIDN'T COUNT" The story of Jutei, who may have been Basho's lover when they were younger, and who remained his close friend, is told in Ueda, *Basho and His Interpreters.* The Festival of the Souls is like All Souls' Day, a day to remember the dead.

8. *Out of Nowhere, the Mind Comes Forth:* LIGHT PLAYING ON CHILDREN'S FACES

This koan is from *The Diamond Sutra.* It is sometimes translated as "Abiding nowhere, let the mind come forth." *The Diamond Sutra: The Perfection of Wisdom,* translated by Red Pine (New York: Counterpoint Press, 2001).

PAGE 94: "YOU TELL ME YOU'RE INNOCENT" This verse is from Wumen's *The Gateless Barrier,* case 30.

PAGE 94: "SPRING RAIN—THE GIRL IS TEACHING THE CAT TO DANCE" This poem appears in many anthologies. A good one is *The Essential Haiku: Versions of Basho, Buson, and Issa,* edited by Robert Hass (Hopewell, N.J.: Ecco Press, 1994).

PAGE 95: Brian Howlett told me this story. Artists often remember childhood epiphanies.

9. Tortoise Mountain Wakes Up: FRIENDSHIP

The account of the friendship between Xuefeng and Yantou appears twice in *The Blue Cliff Record.*

PAGE 100: "WE'LL WALK ABOVE THE VINEYARDS" Excerpt from Alicia Keane, "Botany Bay," in *In Possession of a Cow* (Melbourne: Flat Out Lizard Press, 1997).

10. The Great Way Is Not Difficult: LIFE *WITH* AND *WITHOUT* YOUR CHERISHED BELIEFS

This koan is from Sengcan's poem "Faith in the Heart." Sengcan was the third ancestor of Zen in China. Zhaozhou talks about and quotes this koan on four separate occasions in *The Blue Cliff Record.*

PAGE 112: "EVERYTHING IS SUFFERING" Patanjali's saying, *duhkham eva sarvam vivekinah,* is from the *Yoga Sutras,* nine hundred years before Sengcan. Michael Sierchio drew my attention to it. *The Yoga Sutras of Patanjali,* translated by Sri S. Satchidananda, (Yogaville, Va.: Integral Yoga, 1990).

PAGE 112: "WHEN I'M HUNGRY, I EAT" Variants of this saying are attributed to many teachers. Baiyun is quoted in Ferguson, *Zen's Chinese Heritage.*

PAGE 114: The Buddha's experience under the rose apple tree is a canonical story.

11. The Cypress Tree in the Garden: THE TROUBLE WITH ANCESTORS

This koan is from *The Gateless Barrier.*

PAGE 124: "LEARN ABOUT PINES FROM THE PINE" Michael Sierchio tracked this down. Doho Hattori, Basho's disciple, attributed this saying to his master in the *Sanzoshi*, the compilation of Basho's poetry and commentary published in 1702.

Learn about pines from the pine, and about bamboo from the bamboo—the poet should detach his mind from self . . . and enter into the object . . . so the poem forms itself when poet and object become one.

PAGE 128: WUMEN'S MEETING THE ANCESTORS *The Gateless Barrier*, case 1.

PAGE 128: The artist is Brian Howlett.

12. *The Bodhisattva's Great Mercy:* A SECRET KINDNESS WORKING IN THE DARK

This koan appears in both *The Blue Cliff Record* and the *Book of Serenity*.

PAGE 136: "THE GREAT SEA OF COMPASSION" Excerpt from James Tate, "Per Diem," in *Shroud of the Gnome* (Hopewell, N.J.: Ecco Press, 1992).

PAGE 136: "FOR NOW WE SEE THROUGH A GLASS, DARKLY" St. Paul (I Corinthians, 13:12).

PAGE 140: Rachel Howlett made the comment about kinship.

PAGE 141: LINGYUN'S PEACH BLOSSOMS From Ferguson, *Zen's Chinese Heritage*.

PAGE 141: KEIZAN'S LINGYUN From *The Record of Transmitting the Light: Zen Master Keizan's Denkoroku*, translated by Francis Cook (Los Angeles: Center Publications, 1991).

13. *The Woman at the Inn:* ARE YOU AFRAID OF THIS HAPPINESS?

This koan is my version of one of the accounts of laypeople who studied with Hakuin. Thomas Cleary has a translation of this story that was published in the now-out-of-print *Kahawai: Journal of Women and Zen* in Honolulu in 1984.

PAGE 147: "BEHIND ALL THIS, SOME GREAT HAPPINESS IS HIDING" From Yehuda Amichai, "Seven Laments for the War Dead," in *The Selected Poetry of Yehuda Amichai,* edited and translated by Chana Bloch and Stephen Mitchell (Berkeley: University of California Press, 1996).

PAGE 147: "MY STORY ENDS WITH FREEDOM" From Harriet Jacobs, *Incidents in the Life of a Slave Girl* (Cambridge, Mass.: Harvard University Press, 2000).

PAGE 147: ARE YOU AFRAID OF THIS HAPPINESS? This is by the Buddha, as imagined by Roberto Calasso, from Roberto Calasso, *Ka: Stories of the Mind and Gods of India,* translated by Tim Parks (New York: Knopf, 1998).

PAGE 149: Basho ran across the abandoned child early in 1684. From Ueda, *Basho and His Interpreters.*

14. *There's Nothing I Dislike:* ON AVOIDING BAD ART

This koan is from Linji, the person who gave his name to the koan school; in Japanese he is referred to by the Japanese pronunciation of his name, Rinzai. See *The Zen Teachings of Master Lin-Chi,* translated by Burton Watson (Boston: Shambhala, 1993).

PAGE 162: "WHY DO I THINK IT'S NOT BEAUTIFUL?" From John Cage, *Silence: Lectures and Writings by John Cage* (Middletown, Conn.: Wesleyan University Press, 1973).

PAGE 168: "IN THE *DHAMMAPADA* . . . THE BUDDHA OBSERVES" *The Dhammapada: The Path of Perfection*, translated by Juan Mascaro (New York: Viking, 1973).

15. *The Master Song Man:* FINDING YOUR SONG

This chapter was written especially for the Shambhala Edition. Rachel Boughton helped with the chapter.

PAGE 171: "DREAMING SONGS: MARALUNG'S STORY ABOUT THE SONG: 'MINMIN LIGHT'" From *Songs, Dreamings, and Ghosts: The Wangga of North Australia* by Allan Marett (Middletown, Conn.: Wesleyan, 2005). Chapter 2 contains an account of Maralung's work.

PAGE 172: "MY DEAD FRIENDS" From *What The Living Do* by Marie Howe (New York & London: W. W. Norton, 1997).

About the Author

JOHN TARRANT is the Director of Pacific Zen Institute, an organization devoted to koans, the arts, and spirituality as a creative act. He has pioneered the development of koans as a method for understanding the mind in Western culture. John has a PhD in psychology, teaches physicians and executives at Duke Integrative Medicine, and for many years had a practice in Jungian psychotherapy. He is also the author of *The Light Inside the Dark: Zen, Soul, and the Spiritual Life,* and writes poetry, published in various collections. He was born and grew up in Tasmania, Australia, and now lives in the hills near Santa Rosa in Northern California. He can be reached at johntarrant @gmail.com, and you can learn more at www.tarrantworks.com, www.pacificzen.org, and www.zennosaurus.com.